ALCOHOLISM RECOVERY

The Ultimate Guide on How to Kick Alcoholism
Out of Your Life

(The Alcohol Addiction Cleanse and Detox Guide
for Beginners and Addict)

William Walsh

Published By Phil Dawson

William Walsh

All Rights Reserved

Alcoholism Recovery: The Ultimate Guide on How to Kick Alcoholism Out of Your Life (The Alcohol Addiction Cleanse and Detox Guide for Beginners and Addict)

ISBN 978-1-77485-254-5

All rights reserved. No part of this guide may be reproduced in any form without permission in writing from the publisher except in the case of brief quotations embodied in critical articles or reviews.

Legal & Disclaimer

The information contained in this book is not designed to replace or take the place of any form of medicine or professional medical advice. The information in this book has been provided for educational and entertainment purposes only.

The information contained in this book has been compiled from sources deemed reliable, and it is accurate to the best of the Author's knowledge; however, the Author cannot guarantee its accuracy and validity and cannot be held liable for any errors or omissions. Changes are periodically made to this book. You must consult your doctor or get professional medical advice before using any of the suggested remedies, techniques, or information in this book.

Upon using the information contained in this book, you agree to hold harmless the Author from and against any damages, costs, and expenses, including any legal fees potentially resulting from the application of any of the information provided by this guide. This disclaimer applies to any damages or injury caused by the use and application, whether directly or indirectly, of any advice or information presented, whether for breach of contract, tort, negligence, personal injury, criminal intent, or under any other cause of action.

You agree to accept all risks of using the information presented inside this book. You need to consult a professional medical practitioner in order to ensure you are both able and healthy enough to participate in this program.

TABLE OF CONTENTS

INTRODUCTION 1

CHAPTER 1: ALCOHOL 3

CHAPTER 2: DETERMINING THE TRIGGERS FOR YOUR ALCOHOL PROBLEM 17

CHAPTER 3: BRIEF INTRODUCTION TO ALCOHOL AND THE EFFECTS IT HAS ON AMERICA 25

CHAPTER 4: STRATEGIES TO ENSURE YOUR PROSPERITY. 44

CHAPTER 5: HONESTY CAN SAVE THE DAY 50

CHAPTER 6: NEGATIVE IMPACTS OF ALCOHOL ON YOUR BODY 61

CHAPTER 7: THE IDENTITY OF THE ALCOHOLIC 70

CHAPTER 8: CREATE YOUR GOALS AND BE PREPARED FOR CHANGE 87

CHAPTER 9: WHAT IS OVERDOSE? 93

CHAPTER 10: DEALING WITH TRIGGERS AND CRAVINGS 102

CHAPTER 11: WHY PEOPLE DRINK? 106

CHAPTER 12: ALCOHOLISM IS A PROBLEM FOR FAMILIES...AND YOU 125

CHAPTER 13: BREAKING THE HABIT 132

CHAPTER 14: THE STEPS TO THE ROAD OF RECOVERY ... 147

CHAPTER 15: STRATEGY AND GOALS 158

CHAPTER 16: RETHINK THE WAY YOU DRINK 170

CHAPTER 17: COLD TURKEY: HOW TO GET RID OF ALCOHOL ABSOLUTELY 176

CONCLUSION 184

Introduction

The book provides guidelines and tips on how you can overcome your addiction to alcohol.

Alcohol is a part of our culture since the beginning of the human race. Indeed drinking alcoholic drinks has been a major element of numerous ceremonies throughout history and it is still commonplace even today. All over the world millions, perhaps million of persons have drunk alcohol at some point throughout their lives.

What is the definition of alcoholism and addiction to alcohol? When does drinking alcohol cross the limit of what is acceptable? Which are negative side effects of drinking alcohol? What are the underlying symptoms? And, more importantly do we have a solution to get rid of this debilitating illness?

The first step towards overcoming the addiction to alcohol lies in having a complete understanding of the root of the problem and the root of the problem. Like any other type of addiction, addiction to alcohol is not a result of a lack of reasons. In reality, it's caused by the interaction of several elements that could have something related to your personal mental health, your previous experiences, the sort of lifestyle you lead and the kind of people you have in your life and also what you are exposed to in your surroundings.

If you consider these factors In the light of these considerations, it becomes easier to recognize the causes that eventually make you turn to drinking issues as a method of dealing with. Once you understand the causes behind these issues you can devise strategies and implement measures to limit or even stop, your desire to drink alcohol.

The topics discussed will be covered more in depth in the following chapters.

Chapter 1: Alcohol

Alcohol is a legally-produced substance that reduces anxiety and reduces inhibitions. It offers a range of effects that range including poor coordination and blurred speech. The majority of people who drink is an alcoholic, however those whose lives are adversely impaired by the consumption of alcohol can be categorized as a disorder of alcohol use. Alcohol consumption is typically within a glass in various forms, which includes wines, ale and hard liquor.

Alcohol craving and abuse

Beer is an alcoholic beverage that is made of normal water barley, hops and yeast. In comparison to wine or hard liquor beers are the cheapest in terms of alcohol content in terms of quantity (ABV). Beer's ABV is between 2-12 being the most popular beverages (Budweiser, Coors Light, Miller Lite, Corona, Busch and so on.) with a range of 4 to 6 percent alcohol.

The games of drinking beer are commonplace in universities across the U.S and the growth of craft beers has brought beer drinking into fashion with microbreweries and home brewers pushing the boundaries on the new tastes and flavors that are being introduced. One of the effects from the revolution in ale is that beer might contain higher levels of alcohol when compared to usual home brew Some are as high as 11% or even 12 percent.

People who drink only during social occasions or drink only craft beers are susceptible to an alcohol-related disorder. However, it's evident there are "cultural drinkers" continue to drink even though the majority of people have abstained.

Abuse of alcohol and dependence on wine

Wine is made from fermented grapes and other fruits like fruit pomegranates, berries or pomegranates. Most of the it is offered as red or white with a variety of different flavors. Chardonnay, Pinot Grigio,

Riesling and Moscato are white wines whereas Merlot, Cabernet, Pinot noir and Zinfandel are reds.

The types of wines that are made by Grapes

As compared to beer, wines contain a higher amount of alcohol. The typical dose of wine (5oz) is based on the drinking alcohol content in 12oz bottles of alcohol. Wines are typically consumed at dinner parties , along with crackers and cheese. Its status being an "elegant" drink is difficult to discern the signs of addiction it.

Women comprise 59% of wine consumption in U.S and are the primary people who are targeted in ads that promote the beverage. Women are less musculoskeletal and have less water and when drinking wine, the form disperses alcohol, which means women have higher levels of alcohol within their bloodstreams more than males. This causes women to become more impaired , and also exposes their brains as well as other organs to more alcohol-related damage when they consume wine. This is why women are more susceptible to developing alcohol-related disorders, but any gender can be affected by an issue with alcohol.

You or someone else you care about is addicted to alcohol, and drinks regularly, or is using it to avoid depression or stress, then it is possible that addiction is lurking and you need to seek immediate help for any dependence.

Alcohol consumption and abuse

Liquor is the term used for hard drinks , or spirits such as vodka, tequila Gin, rum, and whiskey. Alcohol has an higher ABV than wine or ale and is typically mixed with sodas, juices, or even water. The average dose of alcohol is 1.5 to 2 oz. Carbonation increases the absorption rate of alcohol-based drinks into the bloodstream. So mixing soda with alcohol can cause a faster intoxication. The lower alcohol content makes them safer to drink, which results in more risk of abuse and drunkenness. A lot of long-time drinkers identify different types of alcohol with different sensations of intoxication. However, technology is still proving this, and studies have shown that alcohol can have the same effects on all regardless of the kind of drink consumed.

The setting in which the alcohol is consumed could influence the perception of intoxication. A person drinking glasses of wine with dinner will more likely to feel a sense of happiness and exhaustion and happiness, whereas tequila consumed at an event with a lot of energy can cause an entirely different kind of feeling of intoxication.

Individuals with a severe alcohol disorder might think that they cannot begin their day without a sip of vodka, or they can't finish their day without drinking a cup of whiskey. Whatever type of alcohol consumed, all kinds of alcohol is capable to be addictive.

Understanding Binge Drinking

The binge drinking subset include those who drink five or more units of alcohol, or women who consume four drinks or more drinks in two hours.

A frequent drinker of alcohol would likely stop drinking his drinks. Someone who is an addict may want to drink through all of the alcohol and may require help to quit A prolonged bout of drinking could lead to alcoholism.

The immediate effect of Alcohol

Alcoholic drinks are an important central nervous system (CNS) depressant in that it reduces physical and mental movements. drinkers might experience a reduction in anxiety or anxiety. It is generally marketed as a stimulant, meaning people who drink will feel confident in an event and less worried about what others think of their behavior.

Since drinking alcohol is legal and widely accepted across diverse cultures, it's difficult to distinguish between usage for pleasure and the abuse. The majority of the time, any consumption of alcohol that causes negative consequences is considered to be misuse. The negative effects of alcohol are:

physical injury or physical injury or.

Reliable relationships.

Troubles at work.

Financial difficulty.

If abuse gets becoming more commonplace, it can turn into addiction.

Dependence on Alcohol

Alcoholic dependence, also referred to as alcoholism, refers to experiencing a desire for alcohol-based drinks and not having the ability to avoid drinking despite the fact that it can cause the most severe social or personal harm. The signs of alcoholism are eating more food than is necessary or avoiding drinking, but struggling with creating a tolerance to alcohol drinking, experiencing a relapse or allowing professional and personal obligations to be affected by the consequences of alcohol, and spending longer in a state of drinking.

High-Functioning Alcoholics

There's a distinct category of alcoholics known by the term "high-functioning" alcoholics. People who are high-functioning alcohol addicts stop their addiction from impacting their lives at work and in their private lives.

An article in the New York article estimated that up to 50% of all alcohol users are high-functioning alcohol addicts. Professors, lawyers and doctors make up an important portion of people. Alcoholics who are high-functioning do not realize they have issues until they are confronted with serious effects of drinking. The potential danger with high-functioning alcoholism is that it can persist for a long period of time , with the person suffering from it not realizing that they're suffering.

Other drugs and alcohol

As it is the norm in our society alcohol-related drinks can be consumed in conjunction with other substances. Like the CNS depression medication, alcohol can pose significant risk when combined with other substances including benzodiazepines and various painkillers. Drinking alcohol by itself is hazardous, but mixing it with other chemicals could be deadly.

What is an Alcohol Use Disorder?

A lot of people in the U.S finish their day with a glass of wine or wine. How do they tell when they've surpassed their alcoholic limit? What are the signs that indicate you've reached the limit of alcohol consumption problem (AUD)?

Drinking "in moderate amounts" means that you should have only one drink a day if female and two as a male. One drink equals:

1.5 1 ounces of alcohol (like whisky, rum and tequila).

5 glasses of wine.

12-ounces beer.

Another method to evaluate the way you drink is to look at the typical amount of drinks you drink in a given week.

Women "heavy" (or "hazardous" drinking is over seven beverages a week or more than 3 in a single day. For males, it's over 14 drinks per week and four drinks per day.

Alcoholic Use Disorder

Dangerous drinking may be the manifestation of a condition known as alcohol use disorder. It's a chronic illness that can affect the brain. A total of 16 million people both children and adults across the U.S. have it. If your parents' genes could put you at risk as well as your psychological and physical surroundings can make you vulnerable.

There are a myriad of signs that could indicate an individual is experiencing AUD. A few of them are:

An uncontrollable urge to drink.

Inability to control the amount you consume.

Negative thoughts even when you're not drinking.

Drinking alcohol in dangerous situations.

Drinking alcohol that doesn't lead to accountability.

Drinking alcohol even if it can cause problems or make the problem more severe.

Inattention to activities that are important because of drinking alcohol.

There are mild or moderate kinds of AUD, and it all will depend on your symptoms. It is more likely that you have AUD when any of the following occur.

It's impossible to relax and sleep without drinking.

It is essential to drink a glass of water to get you started on your day.

Drinking is the only way in order to make yourself social.

It is a means to get rid of your emotions.

You drive after drinking.

Mixing alcohol with other substances.

Drinking alcohol is not recommended when you're nursing or pregnant. baby.

If your family members ask you what you drink, you're not going to reveal the truth.

People are hurt or angry after drinking.

It's difficult to recall what you were drinking when you're drunk.

Your obligations are impacted by the alcohol you consume.

Drinking alcohol has led to legal issues.

You've tried to stay away from drinking, but didn't succeed.

There's no way to quit drinking.

To experience the effects of alcohol, you need to drink more and more.

There are symptoms like nausea, shakiness, sleep issues, and seizures after you've stopped drinking for a few days.

The more symptoms appear and are more severe, the more serious the AUD could be.

The effects of the currency

Even if your condition isn't severe, it could affect your mental and physical well-being.

For certain, AUD could cause:

Memory loss.

Hangovers.

Blackouts.

The long-term outcomes include:

Stomach problems.

Heart issues.

Cancer.

Brain damage.

Long-term memory loss.

Pancreatitis.

A high blood pressure.

Cirrhosis, also known as an injury to the liver.

There's a chance that you'll be in danger, which can increase the risk of being injured or even dying:

Car accidents.

Homicide.

Suicide.

Dozing

The effects of AUD can affect the people around you as well and your drinking could affect the relationships with your family members due issues with anger, assault or neglect and abuse. Women who are expecting risk having a miscarriage. The baby will likely be diagnosed with an alcohol dependency disorder that is fatal, and an increased chance of dying due to SIDS.

Chapter 2: Determining the Triggers For Your Alcohol Problem

Many people across the world drink alcohol in one way or another. However there are a few individuals become alcohol addicts. Therefore, the question that demands the best answer right away is: What is it that makes someone hooked to drinking alcohol?

It is, of course, an extremely complicated question that is not able to be addressed in terms that are easy to understand. Yet, experts have identified several elements that could cause alcoholism. These are known as triggers.

The name implies the triggers force you to fuel your addiction. These triggers, which may be independent of one another, affect your attitudes and beliefs about drinking alcohol. As we will discuss later within this article, understanding the triggers of your addiction crucial in the fight against your addiction to alcohol.

1. Tradition or culture

A lot of people are part of societies where alcohol is part of the daily routine. It could be part of wedding ceremonies, the have a daily meal, or at sporting occasions, there are a variety of rituals that we are part of that require we drink alcohol. These customs can create an immense amount of difficulty to stop drinking because they are integrated into our lives as well as our relationships with others. This can mean that we can feel "left off" or unwelcome in the event that we do not engage in drinking. The influence of tradition and culture is an important reason for drinking alcohol.

2. Domestic triggers

Domestic triggers could include any issue that is related to your family, finances, or your relationship with those who are close to your heart. This means that they are personal issues you would like to get rid of or get rid of. Alcohol could be an easily accessible and swift escape. One of the best examples is the times when you're in the middle of an argument between your family or your spouse or being burdened by the burden of debt. This could be one of the reasons you should consider a drink and put things aside for a time.

3. Psychological triggers

If you're struggling with anxiety, depression or any other mental disorder, you might be inclined to seek some relief in alcohol. This can offer you a temporary escape out of your current circumstances. However, these brief escapes from reality that could by themselves become addictive. Reliving painful memories of neglect, abuse and suffering through drinking can turn into a cycle in the long term, and eventually lead to the addiction to alcohol.

4. Environmental factors

The place you grew up in and formed your character and also your current setting each play an important influence on your drinking behaviors. If you grew up in an environment where alcohol consumption was conducted in a casual, casual way it is likely that you will to exhibit a similar relaxed attitude to drinking. This is especially the case in the case of your parents, or other authority figure displayed an inclination to drink or alcohol consumption, and you could be more inclined to emulate the same behavior you.

This also applies to situations that are not within the home. For instance, if you have acquaintances who drink heavily and you are more likely to be one , too, by connections. That is to say, who you choose to associate with could influence your personal worldview, which includes your attitude towards alcohol.

5. Stress

One of the main causes of addiction to alcohol is stress. If people are exhausted and are looking to relieve stress from their bodies drinking alcohol is among the most convenient options.

It's not difficult to see the way stress, along with the need to conquer it, can lead to an addiction to alcohol. If you're not able to master ability to manage stress and are suffocated by stress from every angle Alcohol can offer some relief for a short time in that it helps you take a break, relax and forget the worries. The experience is often enjoyable and an entirely different experience from the relentless nature of life after being in a state of complete recovery.

6. Pain Relief

A few people drink to alleviate physical pain they suffer from, whether for brief periods of time or over a long period of time. In the case of pain relief, drinking alcohol can result in alcoholism if develop a dependency on alcohol. This could result in further physical ailments.

7. Biology

In the last few decades, research on dependence and abuse of alcohol has focused on the idea that it's a mental disorder. But, the outcome of more recent research has proven that, besides behaviour and mental state biological factors also are a major factor in the likelihood that certain people are likely to become dependent on alcohol.

The studies carried out through researchers from the American Society of Addictions Medicine such as the one above, came to the conclusion that a person's genetic makeup plays an important influence (in around 50 percent of instances) in the likelihood that one is likely to develop an addiction to alcohol. This is in line with an earlier hypothesis which suggests that some individuals are more likely than others to drink and misuse alcohol because of their genetic nature.

The bulk of research in this area places special focus in the area of the brain, and its performs. Alcohol changes the chemical composition of the brain and creates certain "cues" which associate the drinking alcohol with satisfaction. As time passes, these cues become integrated into the brain's neurobiological system and may be transmitted to children. This is exactly that a lot of experts believe that a person who comes from a family that has an alcohol-related history is more likely than other people to suffer from the same condition later in the course of.

But, one of the main criticisms made against the notion of alcohol dependence as a genetic disorder is that it impedes the ability of people to make their own decisions on their own. Because drinking alcohol is a deliberate action, it is obvious that anyone who picks up the bottle of alcohol and drinks it down , does out of their own choice and choice, not simply because they're genetically inclined to drink.

It is widely accepted that further research must be conducted before it is able to be conclusively confirmed that genes contribute to the formation of a problem with alcohol. It is important to note that if you are a descendent of a family with a history of alcoholism, it could influence the way you drink alcohol.

Chapter 3: Brief Introduction to Alcohol And The Effects It Has On America

A projected 18.5 million Americans exhibit signs of addiction or dependence on alcohol, and an additional 7.2 million who have drinking habits which are linked to poor wellbeing and social cohesion. Based on an article published by Time magazine, one of every 25 deaths in the world is caused by alcohol.

Early World History

Numerous archeologists agree that the existence of wine made from grapes dates back to more than ten millennia prior to that and that the various varieties of lager can be traced much further back. The earliest inscriptions and pictographs found on mud tablets and dividers depict the production of alcoholic beverages that caused the consumer to feel euphoric, fantastic and blissful.

In the year around 800 B.C., China and India started producing refined alcoholic drinks. The process of improving the quality of alcohol developed towards Europe around the 11th century. There is evidence of a clinic at Salerno, Italy refining spirits in the year 1100. The term "spirits" can be used to describe how alcohol is extracted from the wine's spirit.

The use of alcohol continued to grow throughout the next few hundred years until the middle of the times , when many religious communities began to create a drink to help their priests and to distribute to those within the surrounding territories. In the 1500s, the word "alcohol" began to be used only to refer to refined spirits and not to any substance created by similar strategies, as was recently utilized.

As one of the primary tasks to create an organization, mix managers of the exchange for alcohol blending discussed the most effective ways to ferment to their students. Since the advancement of technology since at the start, it became possible and much simpler to produce significantly more pure alcohol as well as higher quality.

The beginning of U.S. History

In the early days of provincialization in the United States, alcohol was an alcohol drink that was widely used to relax and socialize. It was a common belief and belief in the time of alcohol that it could provide many medical benefits. It was the Office of the Tithingman of Massachusetts was created in 1675 in order to record any violation of the laws governing liquor in the homes of individuals. It was in 1694 that Cotton Mather, a Puritan Minister from Massachusetts was accused of engaging in illegal behavior in the context of drinking to the point of over-the-top.

At the time that followed the American Revolution, almost no attention was given to alcoholism and alcohol was found to be increasingly prevalent in the early days of America. The most prominent efforts to limit alcohol consumption and consumption occurred in the Revolutionary War, yet with virtually no impact. Due to the poor social situation that followed the war, efforts failed and the use of alcohol grew rapidly.

The United States' balance development began in the late 1800s when a social gathering was held for New England Federalists to discuss about the consequences and effects of alcohol consumption. The most prominent early pioneer in the field of restraint development is Dr. Benjamin Rush. His theories were essential to the creation of this concept. He stated that drinking alcohol could be detrimental to one's health physical as well as mental. The year 1784 was the time he presented what we call dependency on alcohol as an automatic disorder. He developed the basis for what is currently called the illness concept or model of compulsion or alcoholism.

In spite of the considerations the pondering of Dr. Surge, the thoughts of moderation development and the bourbon tax (The Act of 1791) that was later repealed through Thomas Jefferson in 1802, the number of cantinas during the late 1800s to mid 1800s grew in a rapid manner. There were many in such a way that by mid-1800s there was at the very least at least one cantina for every 100 to 200 Americans which included those who weren't drinking alcohol. To combat the alleged growing pestilence, Maine approved the first legal prohibition statute in 1851. Following the demise of this law 12 different states followed the Maine model and changed into dry states.

In 1862, in addition to establishing the Internal Revenue Service, Abraham Lincoln issued to pass the Act of July 1, which imposed another tax on alcohol. The duty was set at 20 pennies per gallon in 1862. Then, by the end of 1864 the rate stood at $2.00 per gallon. While across the United States the prohibition on alcohol would not take effect for another 20 years, but by the year 1900, a significant portion of states had their own laws against alcohol in place.

Present U.S. History

Alcohol was beginning to lose its popularity for being a liquid drink and also for its medicinal purposes as of 1900. The year 1906 saw The Pure Food and Drug Act was passed, requiring certain medications that were essential, such as alcohol, should be designated with dose and substance. Businesses could no more sell alcohol-based beverages as licensed drugs with "mystery fixatives."

During the first World War, a Wartime Prohibition Act was passed to save grain for the production of alcohol for food. This was the reason for the prohibition of alcohol in the 33 states of the country by 1920. In 1917, the proposal was approved and adopted by the beginning of January in 1919 and the Eighteenth Amendment, alongside the Volstead Act, which was adopted in the month of October 1919, began the lengthy nationwide prohibition period. The official start date of the federal prohibition period was on January 17th, 1920. it lasted through it was ended when the Twenty-first Amendment canceled the Eighteenth Amendment on December 5 in 1933.

Different investigations and reports have shown that death tolls as well as crimes rates of the 1920s were staggeringly high, and that was to a large extent due to an alcohol prohibition. A number of deaths in the late 1920s were linked to contaminated alcohol drinks. Criminality was organized and based on the desire to obtain the huge amount of cash generated by illicitly manufacturing, transporting as well as selling alcohol.

Despite the serious negatives of prohibition, as these studies expose, a lot of people do not realize that prohibition reduced the consumption of alcohol to 33% of its pre-prohibition levels and that as a result prohibition, it is possible to and at any time find dry areas across America. The reason why you'll in the present, encounter towns and areas like these is because the Twenty-First Amendment did not only abolish prohibition in the nation but also allowed states of deciding whether to restrict or escheat the transaction and purchase of alcohol. Then, this structure allowed states to grant single towns and districts the choice to restrict or even boycott the deal or purchase alcohol.

After the prohibition America will witness the rise of a variety of organizations and individuals trying to fight drinking and addiction. The most interesting organization which emerged right after prohibition was Alcoholics Anonymous, established during the 1930s by Bill W. and Dr. Sway as well as Elvin Morton J.Llinek. They provided us with the Jellinek formula for assessing the extent of alcoholism's prevalence in the general population due to the possibility of death from liver cirrhosis. The alcohol history is just a brief summary in the hope that it can help people to better understand where alcohol comes from, where it has been throughout the course of time and the way in which people in the United States has battled with it , and the problems that it has caused.

The history of ALCOHOL ADDICTION

It's difficult to pinpoint the exact date when people began to age the berries, milk, grains and grapes in order to produce alcohol. However, alcohol-based beverages (alluded in the context of wine) are mentioned in scriptures to celebrate festivity in strict rites, and even before the arrival that was the time of Jesus Christ himself. This isn't to say that the consumption of spirits which is forbidden in the scriptures is being enticed by the sway of alcohol-related spirits, which the holy text is cruel concerning (Ephesians 5:18 and Corinthians 6:12). The problem of addiction to alcohol has been mentioned numerous occasions within the book's antiquated pages. According to Proverbs 20:1 Wine is a liar or solid drink and brawler. And anyone who is drunk isn't a good judge.

However the Colonials (individuals from during the Colonial Period) from the United States considered alcohol a drug for relaxation and a source of energy. The tolerance to alcohol was developed, provided that it did not interfere with church or work obligations. The Colonials believed that alcohol wasn't the problem; the more worrying issue was the person who could not control his or her desire to drink. The Colonials thought this "shortcoming" inexcusable and any evidence of it (alcohol addiction) is worthy of punishment. What was compared to recovery from alcohol in Colonial Times was "the stocks" (structures which were located in an open squares, that were used to grab the arms and head of the habitual lilies) where drunken delinquents were slapped with impunity.

In the Industrial Revolution, different social issues plagued the new America. America. Social issues, like the needy, indecent and wrongdoing, were considered to be a part of alcohol dependence and strong moves were taken to end the use of alcohol. Alcohol Reform Movements drove an opponent of information about alcohol fight to alter Americans perception of alcohol. Because Americans themselves, believed it was difficult to eliminate alcohol addiction at any time, in The Prohibition, the perspective regarding alcohol as medical problem was established.

The origins of the AA (ALCOHOLICS ANONYMOUS) to combat ALCOHOL ADDICTION

In 1935 In 1935, at the time in Akron, Ohio, Bill Wilson was preparing to surrender to his alcohol cravings after an entire year of restraining. In the same way, when Bill Wilson was about to surrender to his desire for an alcohol-fueled drink, he met Dr. Bounce Smith who was a specialist. Dr. Sway was in immense pain of his addiction to alcohol despite his declining health. But the two of them found that they could not drinking for the duration of a day. Two frenzied alcoholics discovered that they could monitor temperance every day each day, in light the shared experiences of a tragic alcohol addiction. The two, in final, were instrumental in establishing AA (Alcoholics Anonymous).

The rest, as has been stated, is history.

The history of ALCOHOL UNKNOWN

I'm guessing you've heard the existence of Alcoholics Anonymous. It is a group of those who strive to be calm and assist others to achieve moderated drinking. It was in 1935 that Alcoholics Anonymous, or AA was formed. Two alcoholics who had decided to stop alcohol and wanted assist others with the same problem, formed this group of individuals. After 1935, there were a variety of Alcoholics Anonymous set up in various countries.

According to the AA website, which is http://www.alcoholics-anonymous.org, there are more than 100,000 gatherings and 2 million individuals worldwide. The AA clubs don't need fees for participation since they're self-funded through committed commitments. The thing that connects these people is the overwhelming desire to fight alcohol addiction and maintain a calm.

A lot of dependent on alcohol seek treatment by themselves, while others depend to their loved ones. In the same way they seek help because their judge or manager needs it. There are many people who have survived alcohol whose lives were disrupted. In numerous inpatient treatment centers regardless of whether a patient would prefer not to join Alcoholics Anonymous, he is bound to. However, the majority of the time and again, the treatment won't be effective unless the person who is alcoholic remains calm and sane. Many people who depend on alcohol tried to stop drinking at least once before they decided to seek for assistance. Alcoholics Anonymous is for each person who is looking to quit drinking and lead an unhurried life. The program is comprised of twelve phases that help alcohol addicts can overcome their addiction and face against the issues that are tagging in their drinking.

Gatherings of the AA are held across the world at various locations such as churches or private gathering venues. What's amazing concerning the program is everyone are encouraged to be open and willing to participate with others. However, they aren't required to participate unless they are required to. It's much more difficult for people who are new. It is essential to begin the program by locating a mentor someone who is constantly available to help whenever they're in need of help or just need a little help. The main idea behind Alcoholics Anonymous is that Alcoholics Anonymous program is that anyone can simply do it every day at their own pace, and every drink at a time. Every recovering alcoholic is aware that the maxim "one drink isn't enough one drink isn't enough" is clear.

This is why the cooperation's function because the people collaborate to achieve their goal that is to maintain their temper. It doesn't have any effect on the kind of job you have or how much money you have, or how you're getting old or even where you live. It is all unknown. All information shared during these AA gatherings is left by the people.

Recovery is not easy, but it's a valuable. If, however, you're an alcohol user, seek the best support you can get and are motivated and motivation, you have an opportunity to remain in a calm state for the rest of the time. However, you need to alter your way of life; decide how you will approach every day and each hour and every moment in the turn. This is the most effective strategy to combat it. It's the most effective method to achieve your goal of achieving calmness. Alcoholics Anonymous has helped thousands of people fighting against the effects of alcohol.

ALCOHOLISM AND GENETICS

The possibility of alcoholism running in families has been known for a long time. In recent years, precise research and scientific studies have begun documenting how some families could have a genetic predisposition to the illness. However, despite the increasing amount of research being done there are still questions. Do alcoholics pass on their ancestral lines of descent because a youngster develops characteristics that cause an initial predisposition? Or can a child find out how to develop into an alcohol addict by studying their parents and other environmental factors? Perhaps it's a combination of both?

This kind of family ancestry suggests that for families in particular there is in fact a predisposition to alcohol abuse and dependence, and it deserves further study. The family of former President Jimmy Carter has agreed to let experts examine their past chronic pancreas malignancy to identify possible genetic reasons, other families that have a history of alcoholism should think about doing the same.

The ongoing research into the genetic aspects of alcoholism has been focusing on a genetic marker that might indicate an inherited predisposition to alcohol dependence. Dopamine receptors located in the cerebrum produce the sensation of joy or a buzz when stimulated by alcohol. When the D-2 receptors' number is diminished, the addicts gradually increase their alcohol intake to reach that blissful response. Researchers at Brookhaven National Laboratory examined alcoholic "guinea pigs," and discovered that after restoring the D-2 receptors in rodents that were of excellent quality, the desire for alcohol diminished. After the quality treatment had been ended, these rodents continued to drink alcohol.

In 2004 Subhash C. Pandey, Ph.D. Therapist working at the University of Illinois at Chicago assessed the CREB-related quality. This quality produces the protein CREB that is linked to the regions of improvement in cerebrum capacity and learning. This characteristic is also found in the areas that relate to alcohol dependence, dependence and withdrawal. The CREB quality can be found in the amygdala of the focal region that is the region of the cerebrum that is involved in the control of autonomic responses related to fear, passion responses, and hormone release. When we look at rodents in the same way, decreased levels of CREB were linked to increased tension as well as an increased desire for alcohol. For rodents who had a lack of the CREB quality rodents increased their consumption of alcohol to half. Pandey concluded "that the alcoholism or CREB quality is "pivotal" to the feeling of unease that causes alcohol dependence."

Every year , approximately 100,000 deaths occur due to alcoholism. 14 million Americans suffer from an alcohol-related issue. That's a staggering number, and while the illness could also be a factor however, I am convinced that genetic factors are responsible for the answers to the issues of alcoholism and compound dependence.

Chapter 4: Strategies to Ensure Your Prosperity

You've gone through your steps. You've written your checklist and double-checked it and changed the behaviors in your life that are a part of that involve drinking alcohol. You might be thinking, what's next? How can you make sure that you're equipped to keep you sober? After all the effort that you've committed to yourself It is essential to ensure that nothing stands the way of your goal. Let's take a look at ways to alter things to your favor.

Start an Sober Bank:

In any significant life transition you must play with your brain to make you feel more enthusiastic about the change. Rewards for yourself in small increments can help you ensure your success in this challenging endeavor. One method to do this is to set up an alcohol-free bank account for yourself. In essence, each time you feel the urge to drink any type of alcohol, collect the amount you spent and place it in the jar or box you've set aside. For example, if you decide to go to the bar, you can put in the amount you would have spent on an evening out. If you're thinking of stopping to purchase an ounce or two of beer, you can add that amount to your savings account. Soon, you'll be amazed at how much you've saved. You can then spend it to treat yourself to something extra. Take a trip to the spa, pamper yourself with an appointment for a manicure, or purchase some new games or a extravagant electronic toy. You decide which treat you'd like to have.

Celebrate:

Keep in mind that you're not going to get rid of a beloved, old and comfortable companion! Make this change positive and be grateful for the small victories. For each day or week that do not drink, get out for a night of enjoyable sober time or offer yourself some small rewards. Enjoy as much as you think you should as in the absence of alcohol. The joy of each day that you are successful will soon allow you cherish each day you are given and you will realize that you have defeated your opponent.

Try Yoga or mediation:

The ability to calm and center your mind will be an integral part of your long-term success getting rid of alcohol for good. Although it might not have been a topic you thought about in the past, meditative practices will certainly help in relaxing your mind and helping you let off the burden that drinking has turned into. Yoga is also helpful in treating depression and anxiety. In a research study carried out in 2005, the researchers found that a small group of women decreased depression in half, and their anxiety by 30% , and they reported their stress levels as much lower, as high as up to 65%. Yoga can not only help to improve your mental well-being when you are making this alteration within your daily routine, but it also has been proven to improve sleep quality as well as other body aches. This could be a huge benefit for you when you are first trying to quit drinking as you may have an issue sleeping without the help of alcohol for the first time.

Don't forget your support system:

If you choose to stop be sure to prepare yourself to be successful in the endeavor. Let the people who are close to you about what you're trying to accomplish and have them support your decision. Pick people who are close friends or family members and not your previous drinking companions who can tell you that you're not a issue and you don't have to stop. If you are feeling that you're ready to give up or feel like taking an alcohol-related drink, contact them. Visit them to become more connected to them. This is among the most important actions you'll make on your journey. Don't attempt to make it all on your own! If you don't know anyone to ask for assistance There are numerous options that can help you get the help you need. There are support lines you can contact without being identified. Join an online group or locate chat rooms for help on the web. There's no reason to feel lonely during this process, or any other concern.

Keep in Mind Your Reasons:

If you are ever you're tempted, just stop and take a deep breath. Consider the reason you're doing this and review your list. Keep in mind that you began on this journey to improve your health, relationships, as well as other aspects of life. Consider what you felt like after you let someone down when you had a drink or how you felt when you were out of control. If just looking over this list of thoughts isn't sufficient for you, then write additional notes. Do not only concentrate on the negative consequences resulted from your previous actions since this could cause more guilt and feelings of regret about your decision. Release those emotions and write a list of the things that have changed since you stopped drinking alcohol. Remind yourself constantly you made a decision you made and your life is getting better due to it will allow you to keep on track better than any other thing. That's what you want and you will be able to achieve every goal you set!

Chapter 5: Honesty Can Save The Day

Because addiction to alcohol is personal You also need to be able to face it head-on to combat it. Be aware of what's driving you and what's keeping you in the same spot.

What is it that you drink? You Drink?

Examine the reasons why you drink? Do you drink because of one of the factors listed above?

The pressure of peer pressure. Do think you need to drink in order to be liked by other people or because it's the social norm?

Curiousity - Do you want to know what it was like when you were drinking? Are you curious about how the taste of a drink was like?

Excited - Want to feel the excitement? Do you want to experience the sensation of drama and danger? Do you associate being drunk with being sexually attractive?

Feelings of Pleasure satisfaction from drinking alcohol? Do you feel happiness, confidence, tranquility and the feeling of belonging to other people?

Escape - Do you use alcohol to get rid of stress, obligations or problems? frustration, anxiety, boredom and many other bad things?

Consider your motives. Are they worth the negative effects? Do they really solve your issues or are they just creating more problems?

There are many alternative, healthier, and more satisfying sources of joy or excitement. There is no need to endure alcohol for these reasons! Alongside the list of reasons to drink, record alternative thoughts or actions.

The reason You Continue to Follow the Habit

Insecurity. Have you ever tried to quit but didn't succeed? Don't believe that you're in the chance to give up for the sake of. Failures in the past don't suggest that you'll continue in the same pattern of failure. Maybe you're not getting the most from certain things and this book will assist you in that regard.

The fear of Change. People are prone to forming patterns and habits of behavior due to the subconscious (the largest part of our minds) is in search of familiarity.

We are afraid of change regardless of whether they require making changes to our lives for the better. Be calm and remember that the decision to let go of your drinking addictions is the most beneficial choice for you.

Make sure you are focused and envision all the benefits you'll receive in the future.

Unrealistic expectations

Don't be afraid to face your flaws. There is no way to be perfect and nobody is required to be. It's okay to acknowledge that alcoholism can cause you issues and you face difficulties abstaining from it.

Don't be afraid of making mistakes. In reality they can be useful to point you in the right direction. Keep doing the things you need to do even if that you fail at certain points. When you've got the hang of it, becoming an alcohol-free person will be the norm for you.

Rebellion

Do you feel that breaking the habit is taking away your power? No! Self-control is a sign of real authority. Imagine making choices that are truly beneficial to you.

Consider directing your thoughts and feelings so that they force you to take the actions you've chosen to do in advance. You don't have to please everyone, so you must change your behavior. Be in charge of your life and you'll realize that you're the one in charge of your life.

Self-hatred

Are you having issues with self-esteem? Do you see your alcoholism as a punishment for something negative for you, or as a way to compensate for something you've been guilty of previously?

Recognize that being an alcoholic is not the best thing you could do to compensate for any thing. When you are free of your mind of alcohol, you'll be able to perceive your situation with greater clarity and have more resources at your disposal to help you manage your problems.

Take care of your personal problems to be able to perform the necessary actions of choosing healthier options and avoiding tempting things. You should surround yourself with the support of others (whether it is external or internal) through these challenging moments.

Kick Alcohol Out

Keep in mind that your brain is a machine, and you must tell it what you want it to do before it is able to do what you would like.

The more precise what your requirements are the more easy to adhere to your new way of abstaining from alcohol.

Here are some suggestions:

Set limits on the amount of alcohol you consume. You can quit cold turkey and stop drinking the alcohol completely. Alternately, you could slowly decrease your alcohol consumption or keep the amount to a minimum. Set a limit for each occasion, or for each time you drink alcohol.

Find a substitute. If you feel the urge to drink due to of the occasion or simply out of habit, ensure that you've got something else to drink, which is not alcoholic.

Water is the most suitable option, but you can choose juices made from fruits. Soda is not healthy however it's not alcohol.

Get distracted. Keep yourself busy enough that you're not able to drink. Take action on the things you put off. Set goals and meet them even in times when you're drinking.

Make friends with non-drinkers. There are plenty of things to be distracted by - drinking isn't one of them!

Eliminate the triggers. If you have bottles of alcohol in your home, get rid of them or let someone else do it. If you continue to pass bars while driving to work, take the road without bars.

If you drink alcohol because you are feeling a certain way try to avoid it or set a goal to change your behavior even if you are feeling those emotions. In earlier chapters, you have observed the patterns of your behavior and now is the time to break it down and create healthier habits by identifying sustainable alternatives.

Find excuses to not drink. If you're the constant subject of pressure from your peers, create strategies to avoid being pressured into doing things you'd rather avoid. As an example, you can offer to drive for your drinking companions. Make a list of your anti-liquor reactions and practice them until you be able to communicate them to your friends.

The Finish Line

The chemistry of your body changes when you drink alcohol which is why, once your body has become accustomed to the presence of alcohol in your system, you may be experiencing some problems, like the following:

- Stomach upset

- Nausea

- Feeling trembling

- Fatigue

- Sleepiness

- Hypertension

If you are suffering from severe symptoms then seek out help from your physician. He can assist you deal with these. To prevent these from happening problems, you should gradually reduce your alcohol consumption so that you don't upset your body by abrupt withdrawal of alcohol.

Here are a few ways to accomplish this:

Choose one or two abstinence days per week. If you drink regularly, consider taking a few days without alcohol. After a few weeks, you can increase the number of time until at 7 days alcohol-free.

Drinking slow. If you drink too fast, you'll lose all track of how much the alcohol that you're drinking. Instead, take your time sipping and let a standard beverage (see section) last for about an hour. Try to stay clear of drinking alcohol following that.

Drink non-alcoholic drinks alongside your alcohol drink. Make your mind believe that you're taking the exact same quantity of alcohol by mixing your hard drink with non-alcoholic drinks.

Drink plenty of juice or water. Water and alcohol aren't compatible, therefore drinking one will flush away the next. Take more liquids and drink more to eliminate the alcohol from your body.

Maintaining Yourself

Don't let alcoholism rule your thoughts about your self. Your habits are merely a tiny part of their own. Therefore, there's no reason to feel helpless simply because you're an alcohol addict.

You can overcome the addiction - when you make your mind believe that it's possible to fight alcohol, it will be able to have greater strength to overcome obstacles and finding more methods to reach your objectives. Talk to people who have beaten the addiction of their addiction.

The more you learn about their experiences and experiences, the more your mind will be convinced that you can achieve what they accomplished.

Imagine what it would feel to be totally in a position to be alcohol-free for the rest of your all of your life: you'll earn greater money and a more healthy and healthier body, not having to worry about those unpleasant negative effects that you've discussed earlier, etc.

Imagine every beautiful detail. Feel inspired and know that you truly desire to get rid of the addiction to alcohol - we are motivated by our feelings regardless. Take a deep breath and consider why you would like this to occur.

If you don't succeed, simply keep going and don't let your failure convince you that you're not capable of it. In reality, plenty of individuals have achieved it, and you too!

Chapter 6: Negative Impacts of Alcohol on Your Body

What happens to the body

Alcohol is a chemical that is easily absorbed into the bloodstream. This is dispersed throughout your body. Do you remember the time when you first drank alcohol? The first time you took a sip or perhaps your first shot and you felt the warm liquid flow from your mouth to your stomach , and then , after a couple of minutes after that, you felt that warm sensation throughout. After that, you're feeling drunk and lightheaded, which indicates that the alcohol that is in your blood been absorbed into your brain.

This is how quickly alcohol is distributed across different organs and tissues in the body. But under 10% of it is actually excreted via sweat and urine. The remainder is absorbed into the pancreas, the liver and other organs in the body.

Here are a few of the effects of alcohol on the body:

Alcohol's short-term effects on the body

Alcohol can make you feel drunk as well as light and confident , which is the reason why people drink alcohol prior to doing something a bit extreme. It can also alter your pulse rate and breathing. It also increases body temperature that is one of the main reasons that people living in cold climates drink alcohol on a daily routine. The breath will smell foul and sweat. You'll feel full and need to go to the bathroom. A few drink and get out of control, while others drink and fall into an eerie sleeping.

Each drinker is different from one another due to the fact that our bodies differ from each other. Certain people may be extremely sensitive to alcohol while others might not. There are those who drink socially while others drink just to forget about their issues.

Long-term effects of alcohol

Liver problems - your liver absorbs all the damage you inflict when you consume alcohol. It's the job of the liver to break down alcohol but traces of the substance remain in the liver, which results in all sorts of ailments. Many suffer from chronic inflammation of the liver which can cause the condition known as cirrhosis. As scars grow, they ultimately destroy the liver and it is unable to perform its usual tasks in the long term. Hepatitis is a condition that can be caused by drinking excessively which causes the skin to yellow the skin and eyes, as well as inflammation of the liver.

Pancreas inflammation - The pancreas is an organ which produces digestive juices to help digest food. It's also that is responsible for the regulation of insulin and the levels of glucose. If you drink alcohol in excess the pancreas will rectify this by releasing harmful substances. These substances significantly affect the way that the pancreas functions normally. In the end, you will develop pancreatitis which is an extreme irritation of your pancreas that results in the organ's destruction.

If you suffer from diabetes, it is possible that you be afflicted by various issues and may even worsen your condition if you drink too much.

Central nervous system impacts When a person consumes in excess alcohol, he can develop various conditions of the central nervous system. The person will experience low coordination, speech slurred and a poor memory. If he drinks for a long time causes his frontal lobes to shrink , which significantly affects judgement. If a regular drinker is not drinking alcohol, even for a short amount of time he may be plagued by hallucinations as well as other serious withdrawal symptoms.

Heart problems - drinking too much can disrupt your heart's normal rhythm, and in time can damage the heart's muscle and cause serious issues. Additionally, you may experience breathing problems and weakening in the course of time.

Nervous system damages - excessive drinking can result in serious nerve damage, which can cause strange sensations across the body. There's pain in the feet and hands and severe muscle cramping.

Birth defects and fertility problems - alcohol consumption can lead to impermanence and infertility among women. If a woman who is pregnant drinks alcohol, her child may suffer serious complications including cardiac issues as well as developmental issues and birth defects.

Problems with digestion You'll experience frequent stomach discomfort along with gas, bloating and painful ulcers and even diarrhea. Alcohol affects the regular transport of nutrients through the various parts of your body, leading to anemia, lower levels of nutrients, and malnutrition.

Issues with your respiratory system You will experience weakening and breathlessness due to alcohol impairing blood's ability to absorb oxygen that is vital to every cell and tissue in the body. Drinkers who are excessively alcoholic are more prone to developing tuberculosis and lung infections.

What effect does alcohol has on your personality?

It is a fact that anyone who drinks too much is a nuisance. It's possible that you don't know or perhaps you be aware of what your family members and friends think and feel toward you but you cannot avoid drinking alcohol. You might recognize yourself from the following:

Unskilled judgment - you are not able to offer specific advice or solutions to issues, regardless of whether you're drunk or not. If you're not drinking, you're contemplating drinking again in order to avoid stress at work or at home. The alcohol you consume does not solve any issue and therefore you're no longer required to take part in important decision-making process either at home or at work.

A poor memory - regardless of regardless of whether or not, you are having trouble remembering things. You might be able to recall something, but these are fragments of memory that will eventually get lost to you.

Lack of concentration - you're distracted by drinking and, when you're resting, you're sleeping. You are unable to focus on anything since you feel anxious and experience tremors of a fine magnitude even when you're not drinking.

It is a bad time to drink to get away from your troubles with your wife and family. When you're enjoying yourself after a drink and you are unable to make a sensible decision. You criticize others and are more likely to engage in a fight if you're drunk, and when you're sober, you rest all day. The family doesn't have time to speak to you, and may not even know what to say, causing tensions between children, spouses and relatives.

Work and career suffer when you're intoxicated, you fall asleep all day and as a result you are late for work or are tardy to work. It is difficult to make any significant decisions in your business, you are uncontrollable when you're drunk, and this can cause conflicts, discords in work relationships, and sometimes even problems in your workplace.

Self-confidence is low - yes, you believe that drinking alcohol will make you feel more like a man or boost confidence in yourself, but it just gives you a boost. Once the effects of alcohol has passed, you're nervous and anxious to meet people once more and you drink more creating a viscous cycle.

If you make a shift to your day-to-day routine and stop drinking alcohol, you won't only help the body heal from injuries but also enhance your relationship with other people in the process. Make recovering from alcohol as an entire process. It may be challenging in the first few days and weeks but complete recovery is the most satisfying feeling on earth!

Chapter 7: The Identity of The Alcoholic

The persona of an addict is packed with contradictions. Alcoholics are teenagers with a traditional view of life. They are a professional fraudster who loves to indulge and is an self-centered person who doesn't have a love for himself as he is the "soul of the business" and is always at a loss, an individual you can't count on. Finally it is a person who is not scared of death, because he's scared of living. The list of paradoxes could continue for a lengthy period of.

The truth is that in the character of an alcohol addict there are two people. Whatever may sound absurd, it's actually true. In general, we've previously said that drinking is a form of insanity.

The first persona is different for every person, with different childhoods, different intellect capabilities, diverse worldviews, and so on. However, the second personality is identical for everyone. It is crucial to comprehend because frequently it is necessary to understand how a patient in conjunction in conjunction with "specialists," begins to explore his family, environment and educational background to search for the root of his alcoholism. In general the results of these investigations end by the development of the next alcohol-related alibi and a bleak conclusion. Oh, there it is! I was raised in a bad way However, it's not possible to change some thing. Thus, starting over isn't worthwhile.

The reality is that the first person could have had a relationship with any. People of different faiths, homes and the background of the generations. She didn't grow up with her patient, did not learn or earn respect from the society. It is an infection that has rooted itself in the soul and will not stop feeding itself.

The doctor is aware of the person in question very well. It should not be interpreted as a signification of personality.

The second person could appear to be primitive, but it is at first. In order to alter the situation, and to influence the thoughts of not just the patient, but also those within him, as well as the intelligence of the patient will be at play. Additionally, she knows how to sit. She has different views on time. It doesn't matter whether it's whether it's a week, month or even a decade. The demon is immortal. He has no reason to hurry He is confident that he will be waiting for his time. What is evident to us isn't any way true for those who follow that extremely flawed logic. Strength is often used to indicate an advantage; values could become irrelevant or changed entirely.

There is a saying the alcoholism disease is a condition for those who are strong and smart. This may be true in part however is not necessarily in the way that only smart and strong-willed individuals should become alcoholics. It is because the person must use his mind and strength in order to please his master.

It's a bit of a paradox. Many people are stunned: "How could such a powerful person be able to enter into this relationship?" The answer is simple: the person who is second does not ever direct orders. It always appears in a manner of speaking from behind, grows in the first and eventually dissolves. One begins to recognize these thoughts, desires, and experiences as being their personal. The person is constantly confronted with a dilemma to ask why I wanted something and afterwards, I did something different? We would find simple explanations of everything, but now it's simpler, so it's easier to find them.

It is often necessary to examine the superficial judgements of alcohol users and, in a bizarre way that is accompanied by a passion for resonance, and theorizing. The discussion around the subject is so emotional and painful that I would like to skip it altogether or leave the discussion.

The most commonly used response to the question "Do you need to be sober?" Is: "Do you wish to seize me?" It seems that it is best to ask: "Why do you answer the question by asking the word "question?" You will get the answer: "Why do you need this?" As a rule when you ask this question, following the third or second phrase then you must listen to: "Well, that's it! Simply put! There's nothing you can do! You don't have any concrete evidence!" Sometimes a long story is told of archetypes enzymes, and historical references. When you ask "Why do you have to explain everything about me?" You see genuine shock: "How, didn't you know something?"

This kind of behavior is normal since alcohol drinkers are extremely sensitive people who are prone to offending anyone. However, the fact that an person who is a alcoholic isn't always obvious. First of all, the reason for anger isn't always obvious There are times when there are resentments over the bizarre actions of drinking buddies, and at times the person will be offended by the words of a neighbour. Also, even if you don't interact with someone, they will nevertheless have reasons to resent. They will be offended at what's shown on television. It is clear that he only has to take on a few insults to get into the state of emotional mania. A slight vulnerability can be evident even to the sufferers themselves. They conclude that they have "thinly sensitive" to their surroundings, and they are astonished by the "thick-skinned" character of others who surround them.

The most visible manifestation of resentment is a constant determination to feel "righteous anguish." Patients want to feel angry, and just have the desire. When they are angry, they will always arrive at an identical conclusion "With this kind of lifestyle and such a drinking habit, how do I stop? !"

It's a paradox that despite such a vulnerability, patients display an utter lack of interest in the people they cherish. Even to them. They are less and less are affected by the events of the family. They eventually do not pay attention to about what they wear.

Their attitude towards their health, generally is divided On side, some prefer to discuss stomach and blood pressure kidneys, and they are drunk with every day. On the contrary, it costs the same amount to go in the streets naked, consume alcohol to the point of stupor. After a an addiction, many people start to receive a flurry of treatment with drugs to treat the liver, join gymsand get a bit tense. It is apparent that they're very proud of themselves, however when they go back to their binge, the body will suffer an injury that the treatments will go to waste.

The complexities of the mind of an alcoholic may go on for a lengthy time, yet it does not provide a clear explanation of what is going on. The most precise picture can be derived by assuming that the person is in fact double-faced. Then, he doesn't even make himself an excuse to give this information. The intentions of his are excellent, however since the author did not define the purpose, it's in these motives that the way to hell will be made.

For many of my patients, recovery started with the realization that I was another person. I've heard a patient tell me: "I once realized that the moment I feel like drinking I am not doing what my goal. Since that day I stopped drinking. ..."

Tunnel Vision

"Tunnel vision" is a term used to describe "tunnel vision" in the field of medicine refers to eye problems that affect the peripheral part of the retina is affected for some reason or another and the patient's peripheral vision becomes worse or totally absent. The conditions are often present, for example in the case of the retinopathy pigmentosa (Usher syndrome).

In psychology, however the term "tunnel vision" is firmly rooted and, naturally it is not referring to something else. In this instance tunnel vision is defined as the ability of a person to focus on a single concept, feeling or memory that is difficult to deal with the entire situation. In the field of narcology, this term is frequently mentioned however generally when it comes to an urge to consume alcohol. The majority of instances of this expression result in the same phrase: "tunnel vision - when all thoughts are either directly or indirectly focused on the use."

In one way or another The phenomena of tunnel vision can be well-described by psychologists who study the issue of dependence. In analyzing these observations one must talk in more detail about "tunnel vision" instead of "tunnel mentality," or even "tunnel mental state."

Let's look at this phenomenon in the order of memories, emotions, and thinking.

Emotions

For those who experience a dependence on themselves, in the analysis of the events surrounding them and their emotions and feelings, they often, they have to perceive some degree of limitation. When it comes to describing emotions, generally there are a very few adjectives. One does not attempt to find synonyms to provide a more precise description of their feelings. Many experts describe this as emotional deprivation. However, I'd like to point out that intensity emotion can be very high. The "unethical" descriptions of feelings can be interpreted by those around and also by the person himself in a way that suggests "simplicity": "...what nurses! I'm a certain person. They said"Well, that's"excellent!"

The problem: "What do you like most?" Often causes such patients to be surprised. Sometimes, the answer can be philosophical: "How can this be comparable?" Most of the time, it's just irritation. If you study the words of a person like this and you can see the standard scores that these individuals employ. It is important to note that in the set of ratings there are virtually none of the gradations: just three or two definitions for the notion of "good," a little more to describe "bad," and a handful for the idea of "nothing." "How you are" is not usually evaluated.

Memory

The amount of memory is usually restricted. It is not possible to classify palimpsests as a lack of recall of events that occurred during the time of binge. When one is sober in general memory starts with "come in." Individuals start to recall certain aspects of their lives for quite a long period of time however, the memories are splintered. The memories of going in vacation, or when on business, generally are a result of drinking. Sometimes, these are the memories of some intense emotional moments. However, the majority of memories are connected to particularly memorable experiences and are not extend across the course of time. One can remember the exact moment however fails to reconstruct the image prior to and after. Most of the time, these are bad experiences that can trigger an individual's complete perception that they are living a "nightmare" from his previous life. A few people recognize that it's not that bad. However, they will remember that for whatever reason, it's not good. Then, these memories persist for long.

Thinking

This is a review of the current situation. It's been known for some time that those suffering from alcoholism are prescriptive in their judgements. Sometimes, this can be seen as an indication of infantilization however, it appears that this isn't entirely the case. When it comes to infantile judgment, people is able to easily feel a strong sense of sensation, and a connection to an object or a phenomenon. Teenagers often create idols that reflect an "ideality" that they feel confident. However, in this situation the people begin to gather details about the phenomenon, and are willing to discuss the subject, and engage with others who are "fans." These gatherings are where the level of knowledge on the subject is considered during an assessment of social aspects, etc. The primary requirement of these communities is the consistency of the evaluation.

If you are an alcohol-related problem, the person is quick to make a decision and tends to provide an unambiguous definition and then move on from the conversation. Patients insist on providing an explanation of the "essence" in the procedure. They outline the "most crucial thing." Details, generally are of no use to anyone. A frequently asked responses to the question: "Do you need sobriety" is: "What is this?" For someone who is already familiar with the issue this question is generally unintelligible. However, experts are aware that patients expect to be told: "Yes, this is an organizer (chemical protection or code) or." Then the question will be clear, similar to an answer: "How much?" And so on...

It's clear that a conversation like this does not necessarily lead to a thorough investigation of the problem. Most of the time, following an offer to participate in an rehabilitation program patients say: "This is not mine!" That's all. It is suggested to stop this discussion.

Analysis

People with alcoholism aren't inclined to analyze. However, this doesn't mean they are not inclined to discuss what they consider to be the "topic." In fact, talking is a frequent occurrence. It is generally accepted that conversations that are of this type are that have some resonance that is similar to schizophrenia however, without any damaged logic. It is difficult for patients to discuss an issue in longer than. The subject can easily shift from one into a different. It appears that someone has reached all the decisions and isn't at all interested anymore.

Sometimes I had to observe the way someone tried to convince an alcohol user using "on the contrary" or "on other hand" method. He started to explain the advantages of sobriety "Stop drinking, purchase an automobile, build an income, start families." The plan was to move on to an additional step "But in order to achieve this goal, you have to take action first, and then make a decision!" But, alas nobody made it to the next stage, obtaining the criteria: "I don't need a car, I'm employed and I have women who are enough!"

Making Decisions

For those suffering from alcoholism, choices are made quickly. There isn't the desire or possibility to take an informed, deliberate decision.

Patients are attracted to easy solutions. Making decisions are "torn" into the moment: "I will do it today, and in the future, I'll get it later" The majority of the time there isn't any planning of the actual implementation process. The cases appear to be simple or inconceivable. The act of starting something doesn't require a long, arduous process. Most of the time, you need to hear from people who have been exposed to a lecture about dependence "So! All is well but what do I need to do? "

The correct answer is "Go towards the nearest office and there you'll be treated quickly and then you can go to the cashier. Pay and bring the card in with the check."

The above "algorithm" appears to be the most suitable to patients. The question "And what then?" is not supposed to be asked, but if it is it is a reasonable answer: "And then everything will be perfect!" The mistake of the argument is that an alcohol user who has just gotten off of alcohol doesn't know and can't answer for himself"What is good? "What can I do to make it better?"

The people who cannot obtain what they want simply because they were unsure of what they desired. This leads to frustration, despair anger, frustration, and the next break-down.

There might be only one advice: be able to discern what's beneath the feet. For this, you don't need run "run," but "walk." Don't make any ratings, however when you do, consider that your estimate could be in fact overstated or undervalued. Do one thing for one day and make every effort possible within that day, and nothing more. Do not make promises about outcomes, but make promises of actions that will result in results.

Be aware that there's something else in the world that you are unable to perceive because your eyes are wearing blinders.

Chapter 8: Create Your Goals and Be Prepared for Change

Once you've made the commitment to make a change, you are now in a position to set your alcohol goals which are precise and achievable. It is important to determine whether you'd like to stop drinking entirely or if you just need to reduce the amount of alcohol you take in. If you're looking to reduce your consumption of alcohol make sure you choose the exact times you wish to drink and the maximum limit you'd like to establish for yourself. If you can it is best to refrain from drinking alcohol for a drink for at least two days in a week. It is also important to choose the exact time at which you'll begin your journey to recovery. Should it be tomorrow or within the next week? Do you want to wait another month or an additional 3 months? Whatever the date you will quit you should write the date in various places in which you can view it daily. Spend time reflecting on the actions you can take to assist you in achieving your goals. For instance:

Get rid of all the things that could lead you to drink more.

The announcement of your decision to stop to family members and acquaintances. If they drink alcohol, ask for their help and ask that they not drink when you're present.

Be clear about the boundaries you set for yourself. Instruct everyone in your home that alcohol will not be permitted inside your home. Tell your friends and family members that you'll be unable to attend any gatherings with alcohol.

Beware of those who could make you drink again. Beware of people who do not want to support you with your recovery. Prepare yourself for the possibility of letting go acquaintances who cause harm to you.

Take your lessons from previous experiences. Which of your attempts was successful? What happened when you lost control and returned to drinking? What are some ways you could take in a different manner to avoid repeating similar mistakes?

Cold Turkey or gradual reduction in Alcohol Intake

If you're wondering if you are able to effectively reduce your drinking The answer is contingent on the extent of your relationship with alcohol. If you're drinking heavily and that you believe that you have lost control over alcohol, the most effective option to consider is giving up completely. However, if you feel that you're not an alcohol user and you're not quite ready to stop cold turkey Here is some useful suggestions provided by the National Institute of Alcohol Abuse as well as Alcoholism that you can follow to begin your journey to recovery:

Determine your alcohol consumption goals. Choose your alcohol consumption limits. You must make sure that the limit you decide to set is not more than one drink each the day (for females) and less than two drinks each day (for males). Note the limit on paper you can place to various places that are noticeable to you, so that you are reminded of it when you are tempted to drink.

Keep a diary in which you will record all occasions you consume alcohol. It is possible to begin by making a vow to keep the journal for at most one week. It is highly recommended to keep writing within your journals for at minimum a month. Record the date, time the amount of alcohol consumed, your feelings , or any particular occasions that could have led to your drinking. It might surprise you to discover that there's actually an underlying pattern to your drinking habits. You can then choose the ways you can do to overcome your drinking addiction.

If you do decide to drink, be sure that you are conscious about it with a slow and steady drinking pace. You should take at least one hour to rest before taking another drink. You may consume soda, water or any other non-alcohol drink following drinking alcohol to help break your alcohol-related tendencies. Be sure to consume food prior to drinking alcohol.

It is also advisable to spend some time building your list of dreams and then figure out what you can do to accomplish them. Making a commitment to this will help you focus your energy on things that are more important. It will change your life in a short time and for the better.

Don't put off doing what you must do or promised to do. This is one of the main causes of alcoholism for lots of people. The idea of putting everything on "Tomorrow Island" can create anxiety, pain, and stress and it has the chance of leading people back to drinking heavily in order to feel temporarily more comfortable about not being accountable for the things you're required to do or what you'd do.

In an endless cycle of being unable to accomplish your task due to the alcohol, but then doing your best to complete the task, which eventually brings you the alcohol back.

Write down your short-term goals as well as long-term dreams. Do one or more activities every day to help you reach the goals. Every achievement you get will be a step towards the top.

Chapter 9: What is Overdose?

A person's body produces a biological reaction your body produces when it encounters a significant amount of substance or a combination of chemicals. A person's overdose can be deliberate or accidental. It is possible to overdose on illicit drugs, alcohol or prescription drugs, along with various other substances. Most often, overdoses result in death However, the majority of people who been overdosed may be saved if help is offered promptly. Overdoses are the primary cause of fatalities in America. When it comes to drug abuse, there are many ways for your body to be overwhelmed by the substances. But, the most common reason for dying from any chemical overdose is respiratory failure.

Depressant Overdose

The central nervous system (CNS) include opioids, benzodiazepines, as well as alcohol consumption. These drugs are CNS depressants decrease blood temperature and pressure; can slow breathing and heartbeat. This is the reason why these drugs induce sedative effects and cause anxiety and an increased calm and ecstatic effects. If an excessive quantity of depressants are used they can trigger adverse reactions, including respiratory failure or overdose, coma or even death.

Opioid Overdose

Opioids are among the drugs that you can overdose ondue to how they affect the body when consumed. Your body produces opioid receptors in various areas that are located in the brain peripheral and central nervous systems, and the digestive tract. When you take the opioids in their system, those receptors get activated, and the body slows down. When your body is overwhelmed by opioids receptors are blocked, which means it is unable to perform other tasks. This leads to an increased chance of overdosing. This can slow a person's breathing. Certain opioids can be extremely dangerous in that it may take several minutes for a person who has taken heroin to feel the effects of the overdose. However, a person who is using fentanyl may feel the effects in several minutes. The powerful and addictive opioids that are why the president of America declared an epidemic of opioids across the country in the year 2017.

What exactly is Naloxone?

Naloxone is a crucial weapon to fight the overdose of opioids. Naloxone is a popular substance made out of Narcan can be a powerful opioid antagonist which will reduce any effects that opioids have to the body. If someone has an overdose and the situation is serious taking several doses of Narcan can reduce the severityand even make a difference in the patient's life. Narcan can be purchased without prescriptions in America.

Alcohol Overdose

A high-alcohol level occurs when you consume greater amounts of alcohol that your body is able to safely process. The body is able to take around one unit of alcohol per hour (approximated to equal what is contained in one shot of liquor half-pint of beer (or 1 glass wine).

If someone consumes more alcohol than this within a short period of time it is when the alcohol builds up in the body since the body is unable to process the alcohol in a timely manner and a build-up alcohol can be seen throughout the body. It can result in an the overdose of alcohol, also known by the term alcohol poisoning.

Signs of poisoning by alcohol include:

Mental confusion.

Vomiting.

Seizures.

Slow breathing.

Insufficiency in breathing.

Hypothermia, blue epidermis, the appearance of paleness

Factors that impact your chance of experiencing an alcohol overdose are:

Age.

Gender.

Body Dimension.

Tolerance.

Binge Drinking

Drug Usage

Other medical problems

Other risks that could arise because of drinking higher quantities of alcohol than the body is able to metabolize include:

The breathing becomes slower, the gag reflex is more pronounced and a slower heartbeat.

Cardiac arrest can be attributed to a reduction of body temperatures (hypothermia).

regular seizures due to low blood sugar levels

Stimulant Overdose.

The stimulants, like cocaine or meth, are concentrated on the CNS However in contrast they can increase blood circulation pressure, heartbeat as well as body temperature. breathing. An overdose of stimulants occurs whenever the heart respiratory system, and the the blood circulation system is stressed to the point of wearing down.

Signs of a stimulant overdose are:

A stiff or jerking limb.

Rapidly rising body temperature or an abrupt burst of high fever.

A rising pulse.

Consciousness loss.

Convulsions, seizures or seizures.

Chest pain.

Headaches that are severe.

Extreme sweating.

Afraidation and Irritability.

The condition is referred to as mental confusion or disorientation.

Hypertension that is severe.

Delirium.

Stroke.

Cardiac arrest.

Acute cardiac arrest.

Breathing that is abnormal or shallow

Certain medications can alleviate or control symptoms like pulse, blood pressure temperature, body temperature and respiratory disorders of any kind. There are also medicines you can use to aid people who are experiencing seizures or convulsions, like anti-epileptic drugs. Sending the person into the closest hospital quickly as possible can save their life.

Finding Help to Treat Overdose

Take note that treating an overdoses at home isn't the same as seeking assistance from the hospital. Even if the patient appears to be recovering however, there's still the possibility that a relapse could happen or that there is something happening within the body of the patient that which the patient isn't aware of. The decision to take the patient to a hospital can make a significant difference to the case that the patient will live or pass away.

Overdose is a scary term that is frequently linked to death, but it isn't always the case to death. It is possible to live a normal life after receiving treatment for an overdose. However, patients must be aware of the concept and gain knowledge from it.

It's not something that can be done quickly, but it's doable, and not just that, but there's the possibility that the patient will never experience an overdose ever again.

If you're not sure of how to proceed or you require assistance for the person you love, contact a specialist in treatment. They're available all hours of the day, to answer any questions that you may have, regardless of whether it's about yourself or for someone else.

Chapter 10: Dealing with Triggers and Cravings

In the initial few months following quitting drinking, you'll be able to manage the cravings that come with alcohol. This shouldn't be a cause for stress or cause you to return to drinking! If you are treated properly, you'll learn the most effective ways to deal with these situations. You'll be able to adapt to a new lifestyle and manage your craving for alcohol and social pressures as stress-inducing situations.

Strategies to avoid alcohol-related triggers;

It is possible to begin this journey by staying clear of certain places and people, as well as activities that can trigger craving for alcohol. In this case, you'll have to undergo a variety of changes in your social life. Elimination of friends who drink is advised. It is also possible to cut off these friends! Do not count what you've lost, this will be a profit in the long-term.

Practice saying "No" to alcohol drinks at social events. It is common to confront obstacles in your new way of living and you may be invited to an event at which alcohol is served or required to go to a friend's celebration where you'll be served alcohol. Practice saying "No thank you" in the event that you are required to contribute alcohol.

The following tips will help you with managing your alcohol cravings. Strategies to deal with the craving for alcohol:

Begin a conversation with an individual you can trust. This could be someone from the family, friend who does not drink or the person you are sponsoring. This should be a person with a religious conviction.

Find personal distractions such as listening to music, going for walks, doing cleaning or other tasks. This can help you resist the desire to let go.

Remember to keep reminding yourself of certain aspects that led you to never drink again. Always "remind your brain" that drinking alcohol doesn't help you feel better.

The act of recognizing the urge could improve things. Take it off This is known as urge surfing. It's achieved through meditation. This will reach a peak and then fall. When it breaks, it disperses. When handled in the right way, it will end.

"Urge to surf" steps

Begin by taking note of any experiences you've had during the phase of the craving. It is best to do this in writing. Take a seat in a chair at an area that is cool. Inhale deeply a couple of times. Then, you can shift your mind around the body to see the areas where you feel the urge. If you can identify the areas where you are feeling the urge note the details down. Do this throughout a series of cravings.

Concentrate on each zone at once. You might feel either cold, tingly or numb.

Sometimes, it's hot. Pay attention to your muscles. Is your muscle relaxed? stressed? What is the dimension of the area affected? Are there any signs of tension in your lips or mouth? After weighing all the factors, then you can proceed to the final step. This will allow you to ride through it.

Repeat the steps. Make sure you are focused on each one. Jot down your thoughts about how changes within these areas take place. The majority of people feel cravings in the same place generally. When you are meditative about this, the urge goes away. This is the normal way of overcoming cravings successfully. Trust me when I say that it has worked out for many, and it is also a good option for you!

Chapter 11: Why People Drink?

The Neurological Effects of Alcohol

Here, we will examine the neurological effects of drinking alcohol, which could make you drink alcohol.

It's quite surprising that a chemical that seems so simple such as alcohol can cause profound consequences. It is widely believed that alcohol can reduce stress, even if only for a short time and many people choose to drink alcohol for this reason. Alcohol can increase the production of a neurotransmitter referred to as GABA (gamma-aminobutyric acid) which aids in reducing stress. It is thought as the brain's principal inhibitor. When GABA molecules begin to grow within the brain, their impact is very like the one you feel when taking any tranquilizers such as Valium and Xanax. But, GABA is not the sole neurotransmitter that alcohol affects however, there are other neurotransmitters as well. When GABA molecules are increased the brain's ability to absorb glutamate known as an excitatory chemical. It could be thought that it causes increased inhibition but less excitation. This is actually an exaggeration of the neurological effects of drinking alcohol.

The prefrontal cortex is the brain's regulator of the ability of your brain to process information and make plans. When you drink alcohol and alcohol, the function of the prefrontal cortex is likely to become impaired. This is among the main reasons people connect bad and flawed decision-making due to alcohol consumption. When you begin drinking alcohol your capacity to think about things objectively diminishes and the capacity to think from a perspective that isn't your own is eliminated. Another effect of this general dimmering of your mental process is that it can lead you to think that your thoughts are very clear. It is possible that you will begin to feel a sense of joy. It's just a sign that your perception has been confined.

When this happens, GABA starts to slowly eliminate all breakages to the system that makes dopamine throughout your body. Dopamine is a gratifying hormone that triggers feelings of satisfaction and satisfaction. When dopamine levels are high it entices your brain to go back in its tracks and engage in the same activities that led to the thrilling pleasures and rewards that you have previously were able to enjoy. What happens when GABA is released from the brakes that control producing dopamine? What happens if you release the brakes on the car? The car will accelerate. Once dopamine is flooding your system, your brain triggers the desire for a particular reward, for instance, feeling more relaxed and satisfied. Then comes the anticipation (bringing the glass to your lips and sipping) and then followed by an emotional reward (feeling satisfied).

Alcohol consumption tends to calm you physically. Italso reduces stress and judgement. This makes it easier to communicate with people and act as you would like to. Beyond that it also triggers the reward system in your brain that creates a sense of anticipation that something positive will occur. Another neurotransmitter comes into play every time you drink alcohol. This neurotransmitter is known as an opioid. Opioids aren't always found in drugs, but your body can release endorphins, which are internal opiates. Endorphins feel good hormones which are released when you drink alcohol. We all know that opiates can make you feel great, but we are able to get the dose of opiates legally by drinking an alcoholic drink that is stiff. For example the American martini is made up of three 2 ounces of Gin. The more quickly you drink this alcohol, the greater the body releases opiates and consequently, the feeling of happiness.

If you begin to think about the various aspects of an alcohol high it's no surprise that being drunk is different for various people. The sensation also changes drastically from the very first drink to the last drinks of the evening. It can be a bit difficult to stop, particularly when it's difficult to end. Everyone who is stressed out consume alcohol to unwind. Everyone who works to resist them, is able to drink alcohol to ease the burden of their urges. First drink in the evening is very exciting, while the final drink can have an almost serotonin effect.

For example, a young adult who indulges in excessive drinking is taking in all the chemical components in alcohol to change his mood to help him feel better. If they continue to do it for more than 20 years, they is likely to start drinking less of more as the world is filled with worries and anxiety. But, once a person is dependent on alcohol, the primary reason he continues to drink isn't for the enjoyment. Two major fears can lead to people addicted to alcohol. The first is the anxiety of not drinking, the second concerns not being able to quit drinking. One thing nobody realises about alcohol is that the reason for their relaxation can be the cause of their anxiety. It can be difficult to figure out a way to break free from a cycle of anxiety that is accompanied by a temporary sense of relief. But, it is possible to get out of this vicious cycle by using the advice provided in the following chapters.

Common Motives

Motivation is the innate drive that drives us to pursue our goals. Are you aware of what motivates us? It comes from wanting to feel the benefits of achieving your target. Two elements affect your motivation levels as they relate to the importance of pursuing an objective and the level of success you can achieve when you reach your goals. Therefore, your motivation is increased and is dependent on the value you perceive and the possibility of that value becoming to fruition. It is evident that the connection between these two factors is multiplication. This basically means that you will not have the motivation to work towards any goal if the reward that it brings is zero regardless of your odds of being successful. Also, if your chances of success are very small, you'll have no incentive to work towards the objective.

The intention behind drinking alcohol is formed in exactly the same way as other goals. It is mostly determined by the significance that a person attaches to alcohol and their likelihood of achieving the desired result. The decision to drink is largely determined by the value that you attribute to alcohol consumption and the likelihood of achieving this final result. Maybe it's to boost your confidence level or overcome anxiety and release a negative mood, or simply to be more relaxed.

In this article Let us take a closer look at the most common reasons that trigger individuals to want to drink alcohol.

Stress Relief

After a long day, you may feel the need to drink an alcoholic drink. This could be your way of a moment of rest. As mentioned in the previous paragraph alcohol consumption can produce certain positive hormones within your body. Anyone who is under a lot of stress or experiencing a stressful period of their life turn to alcohol because it can help alleviate the negative emotions they feel. People begin to associate a positive value to drinking, and then begin drinking more since it can ease some of their stress. But, the relief from stress can only last a short time. When the alcohol's effect disappears, the stress will be there.

General Environment

Your surroundings can affect your mood, and you may not be aware of that you are influenced by it. Being exposed to a world full of alcohol-related stimuli can trigger your need for alcohol. For instance, ads television shows, TV ads, or movies that promote drinking can make you want to drink. It's possible to think, "If someone on screen looks cool drinking and look cool, I can too."

Peer Pressure and camaraderie

Many people drink because their friends drink. They begin to believe that drinking alcohol is a bad thing and they won't fit with the crowd. In this way they're feeling the influence of their peers to drink in order that they don't feel excluded. For instance, one might feel obliged to drink every time his colleagues go out for a drink during happy hour. This could be an example of peer pressure that is indirect. But, peer pressure could take a more immediate form and more powerful. For example, if you're drinking with your group of buddies, and they begin in a spirited way to encourage you to drink it's very difficult to refuse. You may begin to feel that you're not able to be with them even if you do not drink. Therefore, you decide to go and have a drink. It all comes down to how you begin to view the world as a camaraderie. It can be quite challenging to refuse alcohol particularly when someone is encouraging you to drink it. It is even more challenging for a young adult, particularly if you are criticized because he doesn't drink alcohol.

Accessibility

Another common reason for people to drink is the fact that they drink. They may or might not be averse to drinking but because they are able to drink, they begin drinking. This may seem absurd however, think about it for a minute. If you reside in a place that has no accessibility to liquor, the chances of you drinking decrease. However when you live where alcohol is easily available, the likelihood of drinking increase.

Mental Condition

The most common reason for people suffering from drinking problems is that they are suffering from an undiagnosed mental health problem. The reason they begin drinking alcohol is to help themselves relax and to self-medicate. If they don't have a diagnosis it is possible that they are consuming alcohol to ease the symptoms of their mental health issue in a way that they aren't aware of. Common mental health disorders that cause excessive drinking are anxiety-related social, obsessive compulsive disorder (OCD), bipolar disorder depression, anxiety as well as post-traumatic stress disorder schizophrenia and an history of abuse. When these people begin drinking, they may be euphoric and delight in the relaxing effects. These effects can help ease stress and temporarily ease any problem they may be dealing with.

Release Inhibitions

Everyone has certain character traits that determine our personality. These traits influence how people perceive us. Many people turn to drinking alcohol as it helps them to shed their inhibitions. Once you've let go of inhibitions, your behaviour changes. Therefore, it shouldn't be unusual for people to consume alcohol to enable people to see their behavior differently. For example, a girl may be envious of the way that men get into risky behaviour after they have started drinking. Thus, she could begin drinking to prove that she is just as cool and reckless as men. For a man trying to get the attention of women might start drinking to release his fears, which hinder him from getting recognition. After a few drinks, one might find that the fears and doubts he was battling with are slowly fading away. In both cases individuals drink merely to release their inhibitions. Also, they drink to establish a new image which makes it easier for others to view them in the way they wish to be perceived.

Previous Experiments

The experiences you have had when drinking alcohol may affect your relationship with it. If, for instance, you had fun drinking alcohol or have nostalgic memories that are associated with drinking alcohol, you'll naturally be more likely to drink alcohol again. However it is the case if you've experienced a negative incident or experienced alcohol-related flu (nausea as well as headaches) after drinking, you might not be as eager to drink.

People with an Impulsive Personality

The majority of people who are thought to be impulsive typically choose to take advantage of immediate benefits. They do not see any harm in doing certain actions as in the event that they will get immediate benefits. They'll do it even if they have negative consequences in the end. They begin to place an excessive amount of value on the drinking of alcohol due to its arousing nature. This is among the reasons that heavy drinkers tend to be more impulsive than those who drink light. In fact, they get to the point where they enjoy their impulsive personality.

Social Moral Norms

No matter what you think, social norms can be very stressful. The social norms define the accepted behavior of the community. Social norms impact and determine the perception of value that individuals attach to drinking alcohol. In the majority of western societies, the consumption of liquor is often associated with certain events , and also at regular intervals. It could take such a way that you drink on a Friday night following the successful completion of the week's work. Perhaps a drink at a bar before retiring for the evening. In a way the norms may reduce and limit the drinking of alcohol. If left unchecked one could develop drinking problems without realizing that it has occurred. If you are a regular drinker on a Friday night only to miss the one evening of drinking it could be that you find yourself feeling a little strange. The social norms shape the mind and promote the formation of certain behaviors.

Rebellion

A few people begin drinking in the belief that it is an act of rebelliousness. This is especially true for an era of youth. These people believe that they are breaking norms to show that they're different from others. This act of defiance could be a way to make an adolescent or a teenager, feel a sense of power and satisfaction. It is a part of our tendency to defy norms. For example, if someone asks you to not do something, your desire to perform the action will grow. This is also true when it comes to drinking, particularly when teens are constantly advised not to drink.

To Have Fun

Alcohol is a popular drink among people because they believe that they will are more enjoyable drinking alcohol. When they drink it, they may experience emotions like being cheerful or even joyful. Socializing with friends can be a fun moment. If someone is anxious when it comes to social situations, drinking can help him let go of his fears and have more enjoyable. This is among the main reasons many people drink frequently at barbecues, parties and nightclubs as well as any other social gathering. They are doing this because they believe alcohol can enhance the overall experience.

Regulation of Mood Regulation

Drinking alcohol to boost your mood may not be an ideal idea. If you are able to improve your mood with some drinks, then what's the risk? Many people drink to think that there is something wrong with their attitude, and alcohol can be a way to escape. It provides the relief that you need to accept the situation you're in, which can make the process of overcoming a bad mood much easier.

Curiosity

Curiosity is a typical reason which is usually associated with younger people. College students, teenagers Sometimes even preteens, start drinking due to their curiosity about what the flavor of their drink is and how it feels like to drink. Their curiosity can get over them. They might begin to experiment with alcohol. It is done to experience how it feels to experience it first-hand. If they are not monitored such behaviour can quickly become an alcohol-related problem.

Resistance

If you begin exercising at first, you may find yourself able to run about a half mile without breaking sweat. If you continue to exercise regularly eventually, you'll get to the point at which you are able to run for two miles without sweating. What causes this? It's because your body begins to get used to exercise and gradually develops resistance. The same principle applies to alcohol.

When you drink alcohol is the feeling of a good buzz. It's one of the reasons that people begin to drink in the first instance. However, the body's tendency is to get more resistant to taking in more and more of alcohol. This is why it requires more alcohol to achieve the desired effect. For instance, perhaps you had the buzz after drinking having a martini. After a few days, you may have realized that you require three martinis in order to experience the same feeling. This is as if your body slowly gaining an immunity against the alcohol effects. If you do the same thing for a long time it will build up resistance to it. This means that you may be in a position to drink more, without suffering any negative consequences of alcohol. Because you're not drunk with your friends or family, may think you're not a troublemaker. This is among the most dangerous kinds of alcoholism as before anyone even is aware, the damage could be caused.

Whatever the reason you drink it is important to understand that there's the distinction between normal and extreme drinking. This simply means that certain individuals are not able to drink in a regular manner. If left uncontrolled it can become a compulsion.

You need to be aware of these elements as they are the major reasons for why you consume alcohol. If you're looking to quit drinking, you can't accomplish this until you know the primary motive behind your drinking. Once you know what motivates you it is more straightforward to discover alternative sources from which you can derive the benefit you feel from drinking.

If, for instance, the primary reason you take a drink of booze is feeling more accepted within your social circle You can think of other methods to accomplish this goal without drinking alcohol. Maybe you'll be able to engage in lively discussions or meet them more frequently. You'll learn the best ways to quit drinking in the next chapters.

Chapter 12: Alcoholism is a problem for Families...And You

The consumption of alcohol does not just have negative effects on an individual's physical and mental health as well as on the relationship to his loved ones and his friends. Alcohol can alter your behaviors in ways that could affect the family members of yours. This is one reason to consider staying clear of drinking alcohol.

First of all, alcoholism is regarded as being more harmful and damaging in its influence than other influence, whether internal or external. The abuse of a drinker may affect family members in a variety of ways, based on the first relationship with them and the effects can have lasting and sometimes even life-long effects in their relationship.

Children. Children born with the home of at least one parent that is a violent alcohol user may suffer negative consequences that are focused on personal growth like low self-esteem, frequent feeling of guilt or despair and depression that may develop into chronic, persistent anxiety about being abandoned, loneliness and extremely extreme levels of anxiety and stress. Children who have parents who drink might be inclined be blamed for their parent's actions and frequently get their beds wet often, have nightmares regularly and frequently cry.

Parents who use alcohol may view them as being different from other people and could always make the view that they're not normal and are not appreciated in the eyes of their parent. This could cause the child developing low self-esteem, which will be carried on throughout the rest of his life. The children who they are self-defeating, tend to perform less than their peers, and are less likely to socialize with their peers. It's also been established through studies that children who have alcohol-related parents are less likely to perform well in school as only a lower percentage of them being able get into college than children with parents who aren't dependent to drugs or alcohol. Furthermore, children living who have parents with alcohol or drugs are more vulnerable to abuse from children as well as various forms of sexual molestation, as well as sexual assault.

The negative consequences can be seen in their behavior after they reach a certain age, and they may be unable to engaging in social activities. They could also develop perfectionist characteristics and develop various types of fears or phobias. As adults, they'll be prone to feeling being unworthy or lacking acceptance, which can lead to a difficulty trusting other people. The most common behaviors among adults who have a history of growing in a household with alcohol-related parents are depression, anxiety as well as impulsivity and aggression. They also carry negative perceptions of themselves and this causes them to make poor life decisions and make it a point for people to fall short in their work, socialization and in their families, eventually which can lead to anxiety and depression.

Spouse. It is also impacted by alcoholism. Your spouse may be affected psychologically due to living with an alcohol-dependent spouse. Changes in behavior are always negative. In the actuality, alcoholism in one's spouse is the reason for an average of every year a large quantity of divorces. The effects of alcoholism are not only mental distress , but also physical ailments to your partner. If your alcohol addiction increases, your spouse becomes the your caregiver. This shift in responsibility can make your spouse feel tired or self-pity, and may even cause resentment. The marriage suffers because of your addiction to alcohol. The things that occur to a marriage when you're addicted to alcohol are:

It could be. A lack of contact between your partner and you. When you are becoming dependent upon alcohol the time spent talking with your spouse reduces.

Communication is, obviously vital in ensuring that marriages work. If a marriage is suffering due to long periods of not speaking about the common issues, or even the daily actions of both parties in the relationship The results could be severe. The lack of communication results in problems that remain unsolved and eventually resulting in the problems accumulating over time.

B. An increased rate of stress and anger. In the absence of communication and communication, your spouse may find it difficult to express frustration in a respectful manner or with the accumulation of problems and issues not being addressed the stress could take over and lead to frustration and misunderstanding toward one another.

c.Little to no sexual desire. If you are averse to alcohol, the needs of your spouse are not being considered among them, is the sexual life.

D. Abuse of the spouse becomes regular. Discontent and anger are usually expressed through violence. Numerous studies have shown that physical abuse is incredibly common in marriages in which one spouse is an alcohol addict. Without any sense of responsibility whenever you're drunk, and when you're angry, you are more likely to resort physical violence instead of talking over it with your spouse.

e. Financial problems. This is among the most frequent problems encountered in marriages that have alcoholic spouses. The first priority in the realm of finance is obviously your personal vice. Instead of your earnings or family money going towards more important items such as food or bills and so on, your money goes to on alcohol-related expenses. This can cause difficulties when it comes to meeting the demands of daily life.

Society. The effects of alcohol abuse are not just limited to your family members and children, but is also affecting those around you within your community and the wider society. Indirectly, drinking alcohol is connected with issues facing our the society of in the present. Because drinking alcohol can hinder a person from being able to think clearly and therefore, the chance of committed to crimes ranging from small theft to sexual assault could be very excessive. Alcoholism is also blamed for many issues in the workplace, including a rising absence rate and low level of performance at work.

Chapter 13: Breaking The Habit

Have you ever wondered how to be able to drive and park in a perfect manner while conversing with your companion while listening to that tune that is playing in the background on radio?

One word. Habits.

When you learn the ability to learn, for instance, how to drive, or how prepare beef paprika it's difficult to keep an ongoing conversation with anyone. In those instances you're focused on your task and using all the power of your brain, which means that there is no time for conversation or other things.

Once you've acquired the abilities, it's easier to speak and do other tasks like listening to radio while doing the identical task. Most likely, you do not consider driving any longer or what button to hold while using an electronic gamepad. All of it is up to you and that's because we are creatures of habit.

Habits: the price of living

Habits are the reason why our ancestral ancestors lived in the Savanna back in the day. By forming habits they were able to let our brains be free for other tasks.

In his bestseller publication "The Influence of Habits", Charles Duhigg explained the process of forming habits. The author explained that neuroscientists discovered the brain's structure called the basal Ganglia. It acts as a sort of relay between the body and the brain, and plays an important part in the development of memories, emotions and also aids in pattern recognition.

However our ability to make decisions and consciousness are stored in a different section of the brain, known as the prefrontal cortex. It is located directly beneath your forehead. The reason is that when you are learning something new, all actions are carried out within the prefrontal cortex.

Once a pattern has been learned, automaticity takes over and your brain reroutes the pattern that you have learned to your basal ganglia. That means that when you repeat an action for a long time, you will be able to do it again without even thinking about it. "In fact the brain begins to work at a lower and lower level... It is an advantage since it means that the entire mental energy that you can put into other things" says Charles Duhigg.

Our bodies are designed this way since there is no other way that to have made it through. As they developed patterns, the early human were able to learn complex skills while being capable of paying attention to their surroundings. It wouldn't look nice when they were constantly engaged in building tools or climbing trees until they could not see the black panther advancing towards them. We wouldn't even be here if it was the case.

Their habits saved their lives back then and make our lives more enjoyable. There is no need to consider all the routes you must follow to work or make coffee, or how to manage the washing machine or even how to clean your teeth. All of these are routines that you do them in the exact same way over and over again without even thinking about it.

But, there's an issue with habits. They're not always good and are not on the radar of your mind. They can be quite difficult to alter.

The ALCOHOLIC HAT

How can this benefit you?

It is helpful to learn about your habits as you cannot alter your genetics habits if you're in a way wired to be a lover of alcohol. There's no way to change this. The only thing you can make a difference is your personal choices and the general behaviors you follow when it comes to alcohol consumption.

It turns out that each habit begins with a mental picture psychologist calls"Habit Loop" "Habit Loop" It is a tri-part process.

There is first the trigger. It could be an everyday routine or a different habit or a sensation that is specific to a certain time of the day, place or combination of all. If you are suffering from alcoholism, the cause could be boredom, stress at lunch, visiting at the bar in town, going to your neighbors' home and other such.

Then, there's the routine. The routine is comprised of the craving as well as the behaviour itself. The cue is what triggers the desire. Craving is the unease and anticipation you experience every when you look at the cue. The thing that makes you crave is not the act however, it is the sensation that will eventually leads you to have the glass of wine, which will complete the routine.

The third stage is reward. This is made up of the countless reasons people drink alcohol. It can be stress relief, feelings of euphoria, fulfillment, confidence, or stupor, depending on the person who is addicted.

It is essential to know all about the habits you have because that's where the majority of people make mistakes. Many drinkers attempt to quit drinking because they're embarrassed about it, and then they wonder what they did wrong.

It is not often that people sit down to think about the reason they drink at all, that's the most crucial concern you should ask yourself. It isn't enough to quit drinking just because you're unhappy about it. There's a reason behind the habit and you have to find the root of the issue.

What is the reason you are drinking?

If you do a little digging you could find that your issue might be in the routine, rather as the reward.

It could be just as much concerning the trigger. For instance, if you're addicted to drinking many bottles of alcohol with your colleagues after work. You may find that you do not really enjoy alcohol as often, but you like hanging out with your buddies.

However, over time, you repeat the same action over and over again, it becomes hard to stop right now. It becomes a routine and you're already drinking before you're able to stop yourself.

You must get to the root of your habits. You must consider asking yourself questions, such as:

1. What are the triggers for my drinking?

You must know the triggers that lead to your addiction and it may have multiple things. The reason could be each when you are bored, you resort to alcohol. It could be anytime you're feeling overwhelmed. It could be the time that you are stressed - between 6 and 7 every day in the local bar, or the time you wake up early in the morning with migraine. It could be anything. it could be that your wife is shouting at you or when you're out with people. It is important to identify the triggers that are triggering you and write the triggers down.

2. What is the cause of my drinking?

Once you have identified your trigger, you must determine the most common way you get your drink. Do you purchase your alcohol in large quantities from the local mall, and then store them in your fridge? Do you buy your drink from a local bar? If you're ever bored, you decide to meet your friend who is always stocked with a amount of alcohol in his fridge and you drink it up.

You must discover the steps you take to put that bottle in your hands. Pay particular attention to the actions that are triggered by your triggers and record the trigger behavior and actions that led you to drink.

3. What am I able to gain by drinking?

Finally, you must think about the reasons behind your drinking. Do you drink to relieve pressure from your friends or to relieve anxiety? Do you drink to sleep or drink so that you forget? You drink to be more confident in social settings? Someone told you it's good for your heart which you agreed with. It is important to find the reasons for your beliefs so that you can address them.

How do you break the habit?

In order to successfully eliminate that harmful drinking habit it's essential to know why and the reasons you consume alcohol, so that you can select the best method.

This is crucial since, in some instances you don't have to completely change your habits. If you can alter certain aspects that make up your addiction loop it could go a long way in removing you from dependency. To help with this, we're going to discuss methods you can employ to alter or completely alter the way you drink.

1. Find more effective solutions

Every routine is about finding a solution to problems. Each time that you tie up your footwear in a knot, it's because it is necessary to tie your shoes to be tight so that they will fit your feet. When you travel to work, you're experiencing problems with transportation. If you drink alcohol, you're doing in order to fix an issue.

The cause of this issue could be anything. It may be anything but specific like the ability to avoid withdrawal symptoms, but it could be very specific like anxiety relief, confidence booster and euphoria. It could also be a sign of forgetfulness, and other similar symptoms.

Once you have identified the root cause that is causing your addiction. It's essential that you do not overlook it. This is the issue I'm getting to.

Troubles aren't going away by themselves.

If you attend this rehabilitation program and did not address your main issues. You'll come back to find people who are smiling and they could even get you drunk once again.

The best approach to end addiction forever will be to discover a more effective solution for your issues. If you're using alcohol for stress relief, you do not have to put off the anxiety. You can search for alternative methods to relieve stress like exercise, caffeine and supplements.

If you drink to boost your confidence then you can work on your self-image by studying books on self-confidence, listening podcasts, or working with a coach to increase confidence.

If you find yourself constantly needing alcohol to get to sleep You can consult your physician to determine the cause of the cause of your insomnia, and recommend the best treatment.

If you're suffering from depression or suffer from profound psychological scars as a result of your childhood, which keeps you driving, you may be tempted to consume alcohol. It is essential to consult an expert therapist to manage your depression.

There are many who do not have the same problem that is resolved by alcohol, however, when you are able to identify your problem, it will drive you. Find a solution and eventually realize that you've got absolutely nothing gain through alcohol consumption.

2. Make the triggers invisibly

Another method to break your drinking habit is limit exposure. If you're a person who drink every single time you have working a long day, you should consider reducing your drinking. Consider switching to a job that is less stressful or altering your lifestyle and dietto be less stress-stricken.

If the motivation is a specific place or even a house of a friend. Simply decide to take an alternative route to home that isn't a bar and decide to not go to that person any more.

If you're familiar with buying alcohol in bulk, and you are triggered by getting a bottle each when you open the refrigerator. Do not purchase in bulk. Purchase just the one bottle you need at. It's out of sight, away from your mind. If you can make those triggers invisible, you'll see that alcohol consumption will decrease.

3. It should be a detriment

Although the brain is affected by addiction, it's a disorder, addicts will continue drinking to the detriment of those who are around him. This is only true to a certain extent.

If you make a difference by taking the consequences of drinking to extreme levels, you could urge yourself to end the drinking and opt for something different. There are a variety of drastic measures you can adopt to get yourself motivated the hard method.

What if you had an agreement in writing with your neighbor to pay them $5000 per month in the event that they find you with more than three beers in a single week? What if you choose to consume alcohol that can have adverse effects on you? What if you decide to consume one of the premium wines? What if you hid all of your money with your spouse, meaning you'd be starving when you drink alcohol? What if you told your boss to dismiss you in the event that you arrive at work drunk or hungry?

The ceiling is not the only limit to the extreme measures you are able to adopt. Alcoholism is a serious disease that should be treated in a timely manner. Although none of these strategies are certain to lead to recovery, they can to start the process as you will be forced to regret your choices every time you consume alcohol. The ever-increasing regrets motivate you to take even more actions to achieve recovering.

4. The routine should be difficult

If you're still able to recall the sequence, it's the link between trigger and reward. We've discussed the best ways to handle triggers and rewards. However, focusing on routines could be very effective as well.

Did you know that many people are more inclined to break old habits when they're away on vacation? Yes, they do.

On vacation, people are forced to pay focus on their surroundings. their routines of the past are often impossible or hard to replicate in a new country. Therefore, they tend to adopt different routines and develop new routines.

This is the plan. If you can figure out an opportunity that makes your daily routines difficult then you can make yourself build an entirely new routine for your reward that isn't based on alcohol.

I'll suggest you take a look at the concepts we discussed in this chapter and then give the ideas a shot. Examine your routines and decide on the best way to modify it. The approach will differ for everyone. It's not necessary to imitate your best friend or cousin. Explore your own habit loop and try to change your habits in the next few weeks. In the next chapter, we'll talk about the importance of lifestyle changes to aid in creating your new life free of alcohol.

Chapter 14: The Steps to The Road Of Recovery

Your path to recovery from alcohol dependence can begin now. If you're committed to making a positive change within your own life you are able to achieve it. Don't wait until after you reach a point of no return to make a decision. No matter how bumpy the road gets and as long it takes it is possible to overcome alcohol dependence. All you require is the ability to acknowledge that you are suffering from a problem and seek the social and medical support. This chapter you'll be taught about the seven steps you can undertake to recover from alcohol addiction and treatment.

Step 1. Make a Promising to quit drinking Alcohol

The majority of those who are suffering from addiction tend to begin the process of recovery slowly. It's difficult to locate someone with an alcohol issue who decides to quit drinking for good. It is a major obstacle for those who suffer from alcoholism, particularly in the beginning of the transition process. You might find yourself making excuses to explain why you're not prepared to make the change or dragging you feet in regards time to take steps to quit drinking. The act of admitting that you have a problem isn't enough. It is essential to be able to take step. One of the best methods to overcome being unsure about quitting is to weigh the cost and advantages of your choice.

Consider creating a table to contrast the advantages of drinking versus the advantages of not drinking. It is also recommended to create another table that compares the costs of drinking versus the cost for not drinking. Examples:

The benefits of drinking alcohol:

It aids me in unwinding and relieve tension after a long day at work.

It helps me to be a lot of fun and have fun.

*I don't need to worry about my problems for a while

The benefits of drinking less:

*I am able to be more with family and am able to have more energy for my activities.

It would certainly make a difference to the quality of many of my relationships.

I would feel more relaxed mentally and physically.

Costs of drinking

It takes away my time and energy that I have for my family or to increase my work performance

It can cause issues in my relationships

It makes me feel ashamed, anxious and depressed.

Costs of drinking alcohol:

My drinking buddies won't be able to get along with me anymore.

*I'd be required to take on the responsibility I've abandoned

*I'm required to find a new outlet to address my issues

Step 2: Create and commit to your goals

Set specific achievable, measurable and achievable objectives that are time-bound, achievable, and measurable. If you'd like to achieve them, you can establish an exact date when you will cease drinking. You can also establish a goal of not drinking on weekends at a specific date. You can also establish goals to limit the quantity of drinks you consume on weekdays. It is possible to enjoy some drinks on weekends. It is possible to completely stop or reduce your intake, however you need to establish an exact date.

Once you've set your goals, write down ways to reaching these goals. This could include:

Eliminate all alcohol-related temptations in your office or home

Tell everyone about your goals to ensure that they be supportive and keep you accountable.

Set limits in your daily life. Your family should be informed that no alcohol is permitted at home, and also inform family members that you will not be able to go to events where alcohol is served.

*Take your friends who are alcoholics off the street. As painful as it may be you shouldn't have to be around people who do not agree with the decision you made to quit.

Keep a "drinking diary" and keep track of each time you drink alcohol. Keep track of your alcohol consumption for a period of about a month, and then consider ways you can decrease it even more.

*Sip your drink slowly. Stop drinking between drinks, and drink some food, juice or even water. Make sure to eat a meal when you're out drinking.

Step 3. Safety First

If you're able to manage the withdrawal effects of alcohol by yourself take it on. Some people need to be admitted to a hospital to experience a an uninvolved withdrawal. The decision you make is based on the time of the addiction you're suffering from, amount consumed, as well as the health of your body.

Step 4: Start to Create a New Life

While professional help is a good start, you have to stay clear of alcohol over the long haul. This means you must to reset your life and discover a new purpose for your life. This can be achieved through:

Finding a supportive support group. Find an addiction recovery group as well as surround yourself those who are supportive of you and inspire you to make positive choices in your life. Be a part of your community because it will keep you focused to make the right decisions.

• Taking better care of your health. Begin a workout program, eat a healthy diet and sleep enough. This will allow you to avoid the urge to eat, relieve stress and improve your mental health.

Finding new hobbies and interests. Volunteer your time, or find something that makes you feel satisfied. If you're feeling satisfied with yourself, you won't think about the old way of life.

Step 5: Get Prepared for Triggers for Drinking and Cravings

Six months in the beginning can be the most challenging when fighting alcohol cravings as well as possible triggers. It is possible to control your cravings by using these strategies:

Find something to keep you busy until you are no longer craving. You can go on an outing or listen to music, or do doing some chores. Anything that can help you get the mind of the craving is a great idea.

Find someone you trust and speak to them. When the urge is upon you, grab the phone and call your friend, your sponsor or relative who will support you or a member of your religious community.

They will assist you in staying focussed and committed to your alcohol rehabilitation program.

Consider the negative impacts that alcohol has caused in your life. If you are in the midst of a craving your brain is likely to go back to the positive effects alcohol has brought to you. Refuse to think about the reasons for why drinking alcohol won't improve your life.

Take your time and wait for the craving to fade away. Instead of fighting the urge instead, let it ride across your body like waves. When it is at its peak the craving will begin to dissipate and will soon vanish.

Step 6: Locate Support

You'll definitely require emotional help, guidance and support in order to be successful during your journey to recovery. No matter what type of treatment you're receiving whether it's self-help, rehabilitation, or medical therapy - having support can make a big difference. There are several methods to get assistance:

Join an alcohol Recovery Support Group and ensure you are attending the gatherings. They are extremely helpful as you are able to connect with people who have been through the same struggles and are able to discuss their own experiences with you. They can teach you how to stay clean and help you get through the difficult times.

Get support from family members and friends and family. If you're hesitant to talk to your family members due to fear of being judged or guilt that comes from your past actions, you should consider going to family therapy. This will assist the whole family deal with the issues that stem from the alcohol dependence you suffer from.

* Create a brand New social networking. If you've quit your old friends and life in the dust, it is time to create new connections. You can join an organization or class at

church or volunteer at community activities.

Move to a sober-living home. If your home isn't an environment for you to remain sober, think about making the move to an sober living facility. They provide assistance and a secure environment for addicts who are recovering.

Step 7: Begin Your Treatment

The effects of addiction can be devastating on your body and the mind. So, it is recommended that you take a look at consulting with an expert in mental health care and research advanced addiction treatment programs. Alcohol addiction is typically coupled with bipolar disorder, anxiety, which is why it's crucial to seek out treatment for your mental health issues too.

The most important thing to keep in mind is that treatment for alcoholism doesn't come with any magic bullet. There are certain treatment options that are effective for certain people, but not for all.

This is why it is important to choose a treatment which is tailored to meet your needs. The treatment you choose to receive must be based on your complete life, including relationships, health, as well as your work. In addition, you must keep your commitment to your rehabilitation program. Be consistent with your treatment, no regardless of how long.

Chapter 15: Strategy and Goals

When you've decided to stop drinking alcohol , you must decide how to cut down on it slowly or stop drinking completely. Most of the time people who have recovered from addiction will advise you that stopping completely is the best option and in some cases the only alternative. However, each person is unique and it's about figuring out the best solution for you. If you are able to decrease the amount gradually, you can use the following suggestions to aid you:

Begin by taking a day off from alcohol every week. When it becomes a routine and you feel comfortable, expand it to two days and so on.

Record every when you drink. The mere act of writing the number on paper could cause you to not only see the amount of alcohol you're drinking but also stop you from drinking any more. It's incredible what the brain is able to ignore when it wants to.

Eat first. A large and nutritious meal can help reduce the consumption of alcohol.

Be active. What time of the day do you feel most inclined to drink? Determine your triggers, and create a plan to do something about that. Maintain a calendar that is busy and make your mind forget about a desire for to drink.

Clean out your home. This method is suitable to reduce the amount of alcohol you consume and also getting rid of it completely. It is the same to those who are following a strict diet. If you're eating bad food at home it is likely that you are likely to consume it. You shouldn't feel guilty about the things you don't have. Make sure that every tempting things are gone.

Share your story with your circle of friends. Be honest with the people who are around you. If they don't, they'll be the ones who push for you to consume more alcohol. If they are aware of when to stop drinking does not mean that you will too. Inform them that you'd like to trim down then ask them aid you. People who truly care about you will be able to understand.

Make your mind think you're taking a drink of water, or any other soft beverage throughout the day. This can reduce the speed at which you're drinking, which will lead to less alcohol consumption throughout the evening.

That's fine for certain people, but for others this isn't enough. It's not enough to reduce, you'd like to cut it out. For certain individuals, this is an essential step.

The amount you cut back on slowly or completely will depend on the extent of your drinking issue. If you are looking to quit the habit, there are steps you can take to ease the process.

Step 1: Speak to someone

The majority of people's addiction has been something they've kept to themselves. They're either embarrassed of it or have been hiding it for a long time to their family and friends as well as to themselves. It's an internal battle that many struggle to talk about, since it's a personal issue. While a large number of people have experienced the same experience, each person affected suffers with it by themselves. It's usually due to personal problems. Therefore, speaking out can be difficult but it's an excellent start to make changes. The end result boils down to admitting that you're struggling. When you've done this you'll be able to open yourself to others, and eventually to yourself. I asked a good friend of mine to share his experience with me. He explained that it was about making a decision. Then, he explained that he was at the bottom. He realized that there were only three options to make: go to prison or die, or simply improve. He chose the latter option, and ten years later , he is sitting here with me telling his story. As a friend of his, I'm so thankful to have made that decision and if he didn't, he wouldn't be here with me this moment.

If you aren't ready to discuss your feelings with your family members or friends now, then speak about it with your medical professional. They're there to help you. Many people are able to stop smoking with the help by a medical treatment, even if it's just to help to sleep or keep nausea at the bay.

Therapy is a great alternative to help you quit. It might not be easy to share your feelings with relatives and friends. Certain people find it more comfortable to speak to a stranger who will view the situation and you with a clear and objective view. Research and locate someone you can connect with. You'll want someone you are comfortable with and who can help you be yourself. Most people do not realize the reason behind drinking and often it requires a lot of thought to discover the root of the problem. A professional you can talk to who is knowledgeable about the right questions to ask, and who can assist you throughout the entire process can be extremely advantageous.

Step 2: Eliminate the temptation

Clean your home, your office and car from all temptations. It's a lot less difficult to resist drinking when it's not looking at you from the side of your face. Remember that you're just a human being and that a non-alcohol environment will assist you on your way towards recovery. It takes much more effort to go to the store to purchase more alcohol as opposed to take a drink from your fridge.

Recognizing that getting rid of desires may mean having to get away from certain individuals and social settings. This is perhaps one of the toughest aspects of quitting, as it can be a matter of saying goodbye to places and people which are not suitable for you. Going out to bars with your friends is not the best option while you're just beginning to think about quitting drinking. Involving yourself in a social situation which involves drinking is likely to make it more difficult to continue. Consider that one day it will be feasible for you but initially you're going to need to avoid drinking. Talk to your friends who matter to you and solicit their support. Keep talking to them or looking at them, ensure that you are doing it in various social settings. If you have a group of friends that you never see except when drinking, realize that they are the people you want to stay clear of.

Replace alcohol by drinking water. Water is a source of water of the earth, which can assist your body during the process of recovery. Drinking water can help ensure that you are well-hydrated, particularly in the initial week of detox, when you'll be losing many liquids through sweat. Although it is recommended you drink 8 to 10 glasses of water per day, you may need an extra amount in this period of period.

If you're someone who enjoys cooking and many of your recipes contain alcohol, you should find alternatives for the recipe. It's not the alcohol that is in the dish that's important (because it is eliminated once cooked) however, it is the fact that it's a sign of having alcohol in your home. Instead, find alternatives or eliminate alcohol from your recipe altogether.

Step 3: Be secure

Anyone who has been drinking heavily for a number of years will realize that they are physically dependent to alcohol. When you stop drinking, it can trigger your body to experience several withdrawal-related symptoms. They are extremely uncomfortable and be mild or extreme. A few of them include nausea, sweating, headaches and vomiting, diarrhea, insomnia, anxiety and heart rate increases and blood pressure, shaking, moodiness, etc. Most people will begin shortly after the last drink and last for several days.

Be aware of these signs and ensure that you're in a secure and secure space. Inform someone about it that you are suffering from these symptoms and request them to look in on your condition. Many will attempt to make this happen on their own, but some will require a secure environment like rehabilitation. The first week or two of quitting drinking is the most challenging, and the most likely time for people are ready to abandon. Knowing this and enduring it through is essential. If you've consumed a lot of alcohol for a long period of time, you might need to be monitored medically during the detox process. Rehabilitation facilities are specially designed to serve this purpose, and ensure you receive the assistance you require.

If you're doing it on your own and experience severe withdrawal symptoms, like severe vomiting and bloody vomit, hallucinations, disorientation or convulsions, you must call the emergency room of the hospital. Staying safe for the initial week is vital.

Step 4: Provide Support

Develop a support system and be around people who have experienced or are experiencing similar experiences. It doesn't mean you must be a loser as they may not be facing the same struggles as you. Your old acquaintances are equally important to this process. However, finding new ones to join your circle is sure to help. Keep your life filled with positive people and those who build you up rather than tear you down.

We'll discuss this in greater detail in the future.

Step 5: Get involved

Find activities to do other than drinking. Actually, you can use this to come up with interesting and new things to do. Write down everything you'd like to accomplish, things you'd like to learn and places you'd like to explore. You'll be amazed by how much time you'll have after you've stopped drinking. Start a list of things to do and start recording things each time you accomplish it. Create a reward system place to ensure that every whenever you attempt something new and without alcohol, you indulge yourself in something you'd like. Being active in terms of physical and mental activity is essential, as a bored mind can lead to a higher desire to drink more. Find ways to keep yourself active, whether that's going to the gym running, taking a walk or joining a group or developing a new skill and going to the movies. Find out what activities you can do in your local area and meet people who are attracted to the same topics you do.

A change in your routine could assist as many people are regular drinkers and tend to start drinking during certain hours during the day. Perhaps right after a meal or before eating, or just after work. Therefore, you can change the timing. Plan something different to do go out with your friend, go on walks. Your mind will be tricked into thinking about other things.

Step 6: Be prepared to fall

Don't believe that it is effortless. Being aware of the challenges and knowing that you'll probably make a few mistakes will allow you to not be so hard on yourself when it occurs. Consider every setback as a chance to learn from. If you ever find yourself in this circumstance, figure out ways to use it for you. Take out your notebook and note down the triggers that led you to fall back. In time, you'll be able to identify the triggers. Do not let guilt stop you from continuing your path towards recovery. Speak to someone, write it on paper, and commit to your recovery.

Chapter 16: Rethink the way you drink

Once a person has made a change in the way in which he or she lives, it's time to alter the way that he/she consumes alcohol. This is vital as the way in which one drinks must be altered when a person truly wants to avoid the use of alcohol, and especially because the person cannot be sure that they will never or she consume alcohol again later on. It is essential for them to understand or learn the proper method of drinking alcohol in order to ensure they are in control when they consume alcohol. The time will come when they'll sit at the table with a bottle of alcohol and think about what the best way they are supposed to conduct their lives. If they haven't been taught how to properly drink alcohol and continue to drink, the old habits are likely to return and the dependence and abuse will get into their system and bring back the same problems they believed were a thing of the past.

It's been widely accepted that something that's a part of one's life can't be erased completely with one swipe. It is better to be removed from their life in small steps. If it's an drinking addiction and the person normally drinks alcohol, lets say, twice per week, the first step is to drink the alcohol only once a week for a month. After having it taken each week for a month, it's time to do it three days for a month. If you've been taking it for 10 days over the course of a month, it's recommended to take it just twice per month for two weeks. If you are taking it once a month, it's time to reduce the frequency. should be taking it only one time per month... and reduce the amount again over and over until they have alcohol consumption at the rate of at least every three or four months. At some point, the person will see that they was not drinking in alcohol for the entire year, as he or she did it in a gradual manner and without worrying about the significance about their goal. All in all the above, it is clear that when attempting to conquer addiction to alcohol, the strategy is not to eliminate the problem once and for all and then to reduce the consumption gradually until the consumption of alcohol is less than once or twice per year. Also, individuals must learn to drink responsibly, not to stop completely drinking, but rather to drink responsibly.

However when trying to conquer the addiction to alcohol, they must try to lessen the amount of alcohol they consume by small. For instance, if one typically consumes eight bottles of liquor in one drinking session, the first step is to reduce the amount of bottles down to six for instance. The next step would be to reduce it by four bottles. The third step is to reduce it to three bottles until they can only drink only two bottles during one drink. Similar to the way, it's not necessary to completely stop the consumption of alcohol but instead to decrease the consumption slowly taking one step at each step. Take it one step at a time, little by little, to avoid becoming overwhelmed by the goal to reduce the consumption of alcohol.

It is also vital that someone seeking to conquer alcohol abuse and addiction be aware of the risk zones for when the best time and place to be likely to consume alcohol. They should be able to avoid by doing other things or visiting other places and not being in these danger zones at the most risky moments during the course of the day. If, for instance, you are in danger 7pm after the day has ended and work is done, it will be better to practice breathing exercises during that period of the day. This can prevent them from being impacted by the consequences of not having alcohol during that particular time during the course of their day. It is also possible to do yoga or other relaxation activities in the same room.

In the meantime, if the risk zone is located at the residence of a person tends to drive by on their way back to work, it's high time to choose a different road to get back from work. Experts have stated that getting past the moments of the impulse three or four times can eventually result in the point where there is no impulse at all, until there is no reason to consume any substance. It is not necessary to be strong all day. It is enough to be aware of the strengths as well as weaknesses as well as the exact time and location where they're the most susceptible to being pushed or prompted to re-take the alcohol. It is essential to identify their risk zones, so that they can be prepared to tackle them with proper strategies. Anything that does not go with addiction as something that is hard to overcome, like alcohol, must be battled over. That means that they must be prepared to take on these challenges one by one, particularly in the toughest period of the day when they are compelled to go back to the habit that involves drinking alcohol. Sometimes they might need to take a break but it is only allowed in situations where there's really no way to do anything, nothing to curb the cravings to have a taste alcohol.

Chapter 17: Cold Turkey: How to Get Rid of Alcohol Absolutely

Maybe cutting down on your drinking isn't your goal Maybe you're planning to go all cold turkey and ending your relationship with Mr. Booze completely. It doesn't matter if it's driven by health or financial issues is irrelevant. The most important thing is that you've made a decision to do some goal, and now let's try and make it happen.

Attitude is everything.

A very smart person once said that "nothing worthwhile was ever simple and they're right. If you're trying to achieve something, such as cutting out alcohol (or smoking cigarettes, using drugs, or eating fatty food) it is the very first thing to do is desire it. You must really desire it. If you're driven and determination and determination to succeed, no obstacle will stand against you. It's going to be a difficult trip, and there'll be temptations throughout the process If you've got the positive mindset right from the beginning, you'll have the advantage of home.

Inform people about what you're doing.

There is no such thing as an island and person should be forced to endure a difficult journey by themselves. If you've decided to stop drinking alcohol and you're not sure how to do it, tell people about the decision. Actually, you should tell all the people who take the time to listen. In telling others that you've made a decision, you're increasing your accountability: the sense that you must follow through with your actions after you've taken a step. Tell everyone you can to let them know that you've made the decision to stop drinking; and be sure to inform them of the little goals you're achieving, even if it's that is as minor as 'I've never taken a drink in the last 24 hours I'm not drinking today'. You'll be amazed by the impact a small amount of encouragement positive will do to you.

One thing I've noticed that has been beneficial to many people is to find an organization that can help. You know what you're thinking: "wow! I'm not an alcohol user, I just want to quit drinking. I don't require a whole-hearted treatment session!' However, this isn't what is a support group It's a safe place where you can talk about your experiences with other people who are experiencing exactly the same experience. This is the most important thing that it's well to tell you Nan that you're quitting drinking, however she may not be aware of how difficult and enticing it is to slip up. Chatting with someone who's had the experience, been there and gotten the t-shirt can help you believe that things will improve over time. It's possible that you might have a buddy who is going through the same experience, and could talk with them. If not, there's always support groups.

Keep track of your progression

In some situations, it appears like we're not making advancement: we're simply sitting and bouncing around but never achieving any thing. It's true that this may be the case for the near-term however why restrict the scope of our view to the few hours or days when we feel unimportant and inadequate? Why not consider the larger perspective? In times like these, we require a journal to keep track of our small accomplishments in our everyday lives. Did you avoid going to the bar? Record it in your diary. You went to bed at half nine and woke feeling amazing? Do you write it down. Eat a carrot stick today? Note it down. Write down all these tiny seemingly-insignificant victories for those times that you're feeling as though all of this serves no purpose. So, you'll get excited about your accomplishments and not see it as an uphill climb. Keep in mind that it's a marathon not a sprint, and on certain parts of the way could feel as though there's nothing taking place. However, look at the bigger perspective: you'll realize that all of it is worthwhile at the end.

Beware of your those who drink with you

I'm sure you know what you're going to be saying. You're going to declare "But you've told me to spend time with my family and friends, and now you're trying to convince me to remove my drinking buddies? What's the matter?" But let me clarify. I'm not talking about 'get rid of' in the sense of "never speak to them again, erase them from Facebook and discredit their existence'. I'm talking about'stop thinking of them as a drinker and begin to see them as friends'. If you let your family and friends that you're cutting alcohol out of your daily routine, they'll be completely supportive and take every step to support you in your path. If this means you're staying clear of the big 'ladies night out', I'm sure that they will understand.

If all you share with someone else is that you drink with them', do they really merit being around?

Beware of withdrawal

It's a horrible experience to go through withdrawal. Ask anyone who's stopped drinking, smoking or even taking drugs: they'll all say that the hardest part of withdrawal. The severity of dependency on alcohol, the withdrawal symptoms you feel can range from mild to extreme. They can begin as early as six hours after the last drink you took.

It is possible that you feel angry or you may be struggling to focus or you might have trouble sleeping, or the complete contrary, you might need to sleep all the time. This is the effect on your mind cleansing your body from all the alcohol-related chemicals can cause and the adverse effects are the result of you brain trying control it's chemical balance. There are physical signs of withdrawal as well, such as the sensation of shaking hands, excessive sweating migraines and headaches nausea and vomiting and irregular heart beats. I have known a few who didn't believe they had an alcohol problem, but after quitting drinking for a couple of weeks and then began experiencing certain side effects. It's awe-inspiring, and even shocking to see how quickly our body adapts to harmful substances like alcohol, and then it's the norm.

The best approach to manage these withdrawal symptoms isto firstly, acknowledge that you might be experiencing these symptoms. If you've informed people that you're abstaining from drinking (which I highly recommend that to do!) They may be able to recognize these signs faster than you can. If you're experiencing physical symptoms, please consult your physician or physician. They might be able prescribe medications that will ease your symptoms till they go away.

Making the decision to go cold turkey is a risky and courageous step The first step is often a little frightening. However, be aware that there numerous resources available that can help you along your way. One thing to keep in mind is that you're not the only person who has made the decision to decide to quit drinking alcohol Ask for advice from others who have made the same decision before and do it each day at a.

Conclusion

I hope this book is useful in helping you comprehend and help you get over your addiction to alcohol.

It's time to act on the lessons you've learned, and take control in your personal life!

Thank you for your kind words and best wishes!

www.ingramcontent.com/pod-product-compliance
Lightning Source LLC
Chambersburg PA
CBHW070100120526
44589CB00033B/1010